ANDRÉ

OBJEC

Birkhäuser - Publishers for Architecture
Basel - Berlin - Boston

POITIERS

S IN THE TERRITORY

Andreas Ruby
edited by Kristin Feireiss

6 THOM MAYNE Foreword

8 ANDREAS RUBY Towards a Supernatural Architecture

12 ALESSANDRO ROCCA High Technology, Biomorphology and the World of Objects

18 **SPORTS HALL** Buried Alien

38 **X1** Art Cloning

50 **DONUT** Building Politics

66 **PARISH CENTRE** Hidden Ark

78 **PLASMA HOUSE** Living in (Outer) Space

94 **SPORTS AND ART HOTEL** Harbouring the Body

112 **MM 18-21** Frozen Egg Cell

124 **CAFÉ KAJEN** Wrapped View

142 **NEMOS HOUSE** Secretly Embedded

158 **BLIP** Traffic Blaster

174 **CAST HOUSE** A House to Become

192 project data

194 office info, biographies, publication list and exhibitions

198 biographies of the authors

POITIERS

S IN THE TERRITORY

205-01

349-02

248-03

238-04

702-05

310-06

308-07

322-08

321-09

351-10

705-11

FOREWORD / THOM MAYNE

In his seminal text "Death of the Author" (1977), Roland Barthes crystallized the gestalt of a new era, arguing, essentially, that authorship is a collective process, and the "author" is one who gathers and inscribes existing material, rather than one who "expresses". This text captured the attention of architects, and influenced many who were concerned with yielding their willfulness to more contingent and itinerant forces. One could argue that André Poitiers takes this tendency to an extreme, forcing a disappearance of the architect's hand through the full embrace of computer-aided design and production, and the use of "referent objects" – existing icons in recent product design – as the point of departure for architecture.

The work is particularly compelling for its jump-scale strategy, applying the form of small utilitarian objects, such as computer mouse, water bottle or ice cube tray, to the envelope of a large-scale building. This logic is largely concerned with the production of continuous surfaces to articulate the organization and contours of the parts contained within it. The singularity of the referent's form is maintained with the skin; beneath, the work engages a component system, breaking programme into form families, like cubes in an ice tray. Architectural projects such as stadium, tower, and office building are given taut translucent wrappers to reveal their inner workings, in the same way as the casing for a headlight, computer mouse, or G-Shock watch.

Advancing the idea that design and architecture are more alike than not, Poitiers contains the complex forces of program, circulation, hvac and other building systems within a singular form, prioritizing surface and the desirability of the object. Resisting contingency and adjacent urban forces, the "context" is unable to contaminate (or energize) the work; such is the tenacity of the form. To paraphrase Poitiers himself, these projects don't adapt to their environment, they are superimposed upon it.

The leap of scales from product to building, however, produces certain interesting consequences within the architecture. As the projects move from the anthropomorphic to the iconographic, they are able to resist becoming mundane buildings: there are no façades, the organization eludes plan-driven extrusion, and the envelope enforces a boundary condition. The precision of their making, implicating a series of computer aided design and production systems, is also a happy consequence of its translation from fetish consumer item. In a paradoxical drift from Barthes, Poitiers seems to be insisting upon the singularity of the architecture, its autonomy of form, its status as an object. In all of these ways, the work treads narrow

and compelling territory between object and architecture.

With regard to performance, the projects yield to their architecture-ness, particularly with regard to program. While the design process begins with a "referent object", the spatial logics and building systems are worked out on an as needed basis, shifting the organization within while maintaining the original perimeter form. As Poitiers has himself conceded, function follows form. Within the graft of program to product, the willfulness of the author emerges.

The use of "referent objects" – predetermined and a priori – posits found objects as form generators. This is not unlike my early work, where old machine parts were simultaneously objects of desire and provocations to formal and material research. In both cases, machines, in the broadest sense, are the armatures for the project.

I look forward to seeing this work evolve, as Poitiers will, no doubt, devise strategies for determining which "referent objects" have most potential, yielding even greater unanticipated transformations and consequences in the architecture. I have yet to see the spaces that result in this strategy; although I trust that they are equally interesting as those aspects described above, sectional views and interior renderings are conspicuously absent. It is as if the autonomy of the object is not even to be broken for the sake of a section cut or interior view. It would be most interesting to me and perhaps most important to Poitiers' research to hone the potentials of spatial configurations and qualities, discovering the interiority of his objects as they are occupied and inhabited.

TOWARDS A SUPERNATURAL ARCHITECTURE / ANDREAS R

As the result of a strange metaphysics, the word "realize" is synonymous with "building" in the language of architecture. This would suggest that unbuilt architecture is a deficiency symptom, mere vision and imagination, without any substantial proof of its existence. Architecture has had to defend itself against this dichotomy of being and not-being for at least the last two centuries. This resistance can be traced back a long way, extending from Piranesi via Friedrich Kiessler to Superstudio and Archigram. This conflict between Utopia and reality seems to be disappearing with the advent of the computer. It is being replaced by a space with potential, potential, in which architecture can investigate its reality without ever having to face the question of built or unbuilt.

André Poitiers is one of the few German architects who address this new space with potential. The fact that the majority of the 11 projects presented in this book are still unbuilt makes it clear that he is concerned with a type of architecture that gives priority to the applied exploration of its future position, as opposed to the short-term fulfilment of the interests of today's developers. For him architecture has to contain a kind of research into fundamentals of the kind that is also customary in industry, where considerable resources are reserved for Research & Development, so that continuous innovation is possible. In this sense several key research points can be identified in Poitiers' architecture, and they will be described below.

SUPER-OBJECTISM AS A CRITIQUE AND TRANSGRESSION OF CONTEXTUALISM The marked object-quality and volumetric isolation of Poitiers' projects seem like incredible anachronisms in the light of the urbanistic arguments of the last three decades. They withdraw almost completely from the all-embracing consensus that started with Postmodernism's horror at the "terrifying beauty of the 20th century" (Rem Koolhaas) and marked the architectural solitaire with the stigma of being anti-urban. As an epiphenomenon of Modernism's open urban planning it continued to advance to target status in the major rollback of the European City represented by urban repair and contextualism. From then on, architecture was "urbanly correct" only if it was devoutly arranged within a block structure. A fatal fusion of architecture and urban design that can be read in an exemplary way from the conceptual impoverishment of Critical Reconstruction so that it became Uncritical Retrovision: Though one can hardly tell from the built-to-death streetscapes of the new Berlin, the catalogue of requirements defined by Josef Paul Kleihues for IBA did not only contain, firstly, the reconstruction of destroyed urban spaces and, secondly, the continuation of historic block structures, but thirdly, the addition of new elements that make a deliberate stand against the past as well.

This third requirement may have been very quickly eliminated in the reunified Berlin boom, but conversely it gained proportionally in significance in contemporary architecture in general – examples extend from Deconstructivism's splintering sculptures to New Minimalism's introverted boxes and topological architecture's monadic Blobs.

André Poitiers' architecture also occupies this conceptual territory. Its pointed strangeness and distance vis-à-vis its direct physical surroundings want to work against the entropy of contextualism: not more of the same, but introducing deliberate differences that also sharpen awareness of the surroundings and letting distinctions emerge in their apparent sameness. To this extent the super-objects function as necessary perception catalysts for the "generic city", interrupting the cacophony of its boredom with precisely placed accents.

For this reason, Poitiers' architecture is not anti-contextual either. It is just that it does not see the context from the past, but projects it into the future. Viewed like this, context is not something that has been concluded, but the subject of constant re-editing. The question is no longer how a new project is compatible with its context as formed over the centuries, but how will the project have changed its context in say fifty years, when the former has long become part of the latter. Ultimately a relationship is built up between object and space, for which reason the label UFO (Unidentified Flying Object) is not really applicable to Poitiers' architecture. It is more about ILOs: Identifiable Landed Objects.

CRITIQUE OF ARCHITECTURAL OBJECT MORPHING IN INFRASTRUCTURALISM But Poitiers' position cannot be explained within the simple avant-garde scheme of opposition to the status quo: the object-nature of his work is not just resistance to the revisionism of Postmodernism and its unpleasant after-effects. Ultimately his architecture is just as incompatible with Infrastructuralism, which represents another way, essentially introduced by Rem Koolhaas, of criticizing the urban planning of Modernism. After the situationist urban planning ideas of Guy Debord and Constant, and the CIAM criticism that came from TEAM X and Peter and Alison Smithson, Rem Koolhaas demanded a synergetic linking of architecture (figure) and city (ground) that was realized in his own work first in the Kunsthal in Rotterdam and later, though this project was not realized, in the Bibliothèques de Jussieu in Paris. Here the building is seen as the culmination and extension of urban space, and not as an object that this space excludes. This is why streets are taken up from the urban space and continued inside the building, reinterpreted as access structures for it. Thus the route from the Museum Park transforms itself into the internal ramp sequence of the Kunsthal, like the Jussieu "boulevard intérieur", which Koolhaas uses to turn Haussmann's boulevard into the serpentine levels of a topological landscape inside the library. The street gets longer and multiplies in the horizontal planes of the buildings and creates the architectural space from the structures of the city.

This understanding of architecture, which develops from the physical structure of its surroundings (not the historical structure, as in Contextualism) became the key to the current avant-garde approach to urbanism in the nineties. It is used by architects of the middle generation like Zaha Hadid, for example, who removes the contradiction between building and ground in the spatial complexity of her plate-tectonic landscapes. But it is even more strongly present in architects of the younger generation like Foreign Office Architects, Reiser & Umemoto or UN Studio/ Van Berkel & Bos. They are even more interested than Koolhaas and Hadid in transforming urban landscape into building fluidly. The building is then seen much more as landscape than as object. The kinetic energy of urban space should be able to flow into the built space as seamlessly as possible. This explains the significance of "morphing" and "continuous surfaces" as theoretical lead paradigms of the kind that were set in the nineties in the academic context of the Architectural Association in London and Columbia University New York in particular.

DEFINING POSITION AND DIFFERENTIATION The formal appearance of Poitiers' architecture is diametrically opposed to this trend. To a certain extent it falls between all stools, in that it is located on a blank space on the architectural map between the contextualist retro-garde and the infrastructuralist avant-garde. Poitiers makes it clear that he is remarkably determined to detach himself from the Zeitgeist, and this is obviously very precisely motivated. But the reason why does not emerge very clearly against the background of today's discussions. It has to be grounded and above all conveyed by rigorous theoretical analysis. Otherwise its special qualities threaten to be swamped by a superficial similarity with other practices that tend to be found more in the field of Corporate Architecture. One of Poitiers' architectural leitmotifs, the ideal body glowing from within, with an extraterrestrial aura emanating seductively into its surroundings, is applied in that context just as serially as the codes of his graphic presentation – elaborate renderings of gleaming bodies of light against a black background. In the eighties and nineties hightech architecture was seen largely as a prestigious architectural language for the headquarters of global concerns, but now this role is increasingly being taken over by a high-image architecture that recasts the visionary vocabulary of Pop Architecture (Archigram) in the service of Corporate Architecture with a futuristic touch. This is an avant-garde amortization restricted largely to form – while programmatic ambitions based on redefining social and cultural norms disappear silently as largely economically determined developer scenarios are fulfilled. While the Archigram principle of "Plug-ins" is enjoying a dubious comeback in cosmetically enhanced shopping malls, airports, worlds of entertainment and the like, Poitiers tends to use it as a diagrammatic module that can be exploited to create new links between architecture and urbanism, figure and ground, interior and exterior world. In his thinking, every architectural statement has to be an urbanism statement as well, as shown by his Plasma House, for example: intended architecturally as a self-contained and self-maintaining system, in urban terms it functions as a basic building element in the network-like interlinking of building, infrastructure and town.

DESIGN AS AN ARCHITECTURAL REFERENCE PARADIGM Poitiers allots a central role to his notion of design. Ultimately he would like to practise architecture as if it were industrial and product design, and so for this reason he does not draw a systematic border between the two fields. He would not just like to produce architecture in the way that industrial design is produced today – in other words with the aid of integrated CAD/CAM technologies, as used in the car industry's rapid prototyping or in Consumer Design. And again, Poitiers is not just interested in design because of the much higher innovation rates in material and manufacturing research, which are unequalled in architecture. Above all, design takes Poitiers to new (proto-)typologies (this is where the motif of the self-contained, self-regulating object comes from) and the new user habits resulting from this. And the redefinition of context in Poitiers' architecture that has already been mentioned can only be explained in terms of this meaning of the design paradigm, and it is only on this conceptual basis that the reality of its interaction with the context can be proved. Unlike the above examples, this interaction is not realized by bringing everything into line typologically (Contextualism) or by topological manipulation of the ground (Infrastructuralism), but in a much more performative way. In this context the theme of substructures has a crucial role to play. Substructures are needed for Poitiers' ILOs because of the enlargement of scale from design to architecture. A small design object like a soap container can be handled and used in its self-contained form. But if this design typology is scaled up to a building, substructures are needed that make it possible for architecture and its surroundings to enter into a metabolic relationship: entrances, emergency exits, openings for lighting, ventilation, deliveries etc. Rather like the gangways between an aircraft and the arrivals hall, they represent a kind of infrastructural interface – or infraface – that mediates between the pure and ideal quality of the designed object and the contingency of its surroundings – and thus makes it useful in the first place. This infraface imposes a tendential restriction on the ideal quality of the architectural body, and for this reason the question of how it is ultimately conveyed in an architecture of precise geometry like Poitiers' (for example, concealed, embedded, demonstrated) is critically important.

ARTIFICIAL ORGANICS AS FORMAL LANGUAGE This raises additional questions about connections between form, construction and typology. Combining an organically formed body and a cubic envelope is typical of many of Poitiers' projects. The contrast between hard and soft could not be clearer. And yet their qualities seem to change because they relate to each other, producing paradoxical meanings: the soft form loses the connotations of the organic in the sense used by Häring and Scharoun, and takes on an essentially technoid colouring because it has been placed in a hightech envelope. The contradictory nature of this artificially organic quality has a great deal to do with the conceptual transformation that basic Western concepts like "nature" and "technology" are undergoing at the moment in the context of scientific and social change. Some of Poitiers' projects are already starting to indicate the consequences these changes will bring for architecture (for example in relation to Häring's concept of the "house-body" (Wohnleib) or the concept of "metabolism" between a building and the eco-system). And if some of his projects really are built soon, then we can look forward to the reality test with a degree of eagerness.

HIGH TECHNOLOGY, BIOMORPHOLOGY AND THE WORLD O

André Poitiers's adventure in design has been one of experimentation, an experimentation in which he has pursued difficult objectives and pushed himself to the edge of known territory. The expertise is there, acquired in the studio of Norman Foster, but his dream has invaded the territory of architecture and generated intentionally provocative figures, witnesses to an illusion in which the appearance, the simulacrum, puts up a resistance to the reality and substance of construction. It could be described as a voluntary exile, an abstinence sought out as a ritual of purification, a redemption required in order to construct a personal and original way forward.

His teacher, Norman Foster, had been the avenger of the avant-garde in the sixties. Buoyed up by the enthusiasm of Reyner Banham, Alison and Peter Smithson and the Independent Group, the radical line taken by Archigram and Cedric Price had been driven into a corner by the technocratic rationalization of Foster and his famous Willis-Faber-Dumas Insurance Offices at Ipswich. If Foster was "papa", a virile model of efficiency, rationality and performance, of perfect professionalism, Archigram were the grandpas, a liberating example of imagination in power, revolutionaries capable of playing with and dreaming the impossible, of being uneconomical and pop, challenging the established order. And there was a third important presence in the family album, Jan Kaplicky. Project director of the Foster studio and founder of Future Systems, Kaplicky challenged Foster's logic, opposing it with an "architecture of desire" in which technology was the support for a phantasmagoria with a predominantly organic, if not explicitly sexual content.

"Future Systems stands for the continuity between the pneumatic structures (environmental bubbles) of the sixties, all the way to the computer-generated, fluid, compact forms of the present." Poitiers also rejected the minimalist technicism of his master in order to look for room for maneuver, and for error, which he considered vital. In the meantime the fifties and sixties returned in grand style and invaded, with more or less retro accents, the world of industrial design. Streamlining came back, with characteristic speed, in the Brancusian elegance of Marc Newson, in the dark and punk drift of Nigel Coates and, above all, in the joyful prêt-à-porter of Philippe Starck, the high priest of postmodern hedonism. In Britain the hightech of Foster, Richard Rogers, Nicholas Grimshaw and Michael Hopkins had become the official style of the business and cultural establishment, and their possible antagonists – first of all David Chipperfield, and then Tony Fretton, Caruso and St. John, Sergison Bates, Florian Beigel – dithered between the memory of 9H and the search for a new kind of art. The energy and "insistence on the new" of the Architectural Association were transplanted, through the efforts of that unconventional gardener Rem Koolhaas, to the Netherlands. With Aldo van Eyck dethroned, Koolhaas became the patron of a new energetic and cynical generation that ranged freely through the abandoned territories of the avant-garde. But even his not all that explicit revision of the modern was unmasked and overtaken. Classical modernism lost even its last romantically archeological appeal and was reduced, as Reyner Banham had put it, to a not very inspiring "series of rectangular coincidences", while Constant and Situationism came back into vogue. The new Dutch – MVRDV, West 8 / Adriaan Geuze, Koen van Velsen, Nox, NL Architects, Oosterhuis, Bosch Haslett – became raiders of the lost ark amid the century's avant-garde movements.

PURE POP FOR NEW PEOPLE Returning from London to Hamburg, Poitiers picked his own, original, way through this incessant dance, this race driven by futuristic and iconoclastic impetus. Technology and New Pop seem to have been the hardware and software of his path; on the one hand Foster, on the other the nonconformist and kaleidoscopic world of the fanciful sixties with its updates. The accounts were settled with Foster right from the start. His first important commission, the Sporthalle in Halstenbek (1994-97), is the only building Poitiers has realized and also the only one of his projects that develops a classic hightech theme, the self-supporting vaulted roof of maximum lightness, and maximum transparence. In fact the Sporthalle is an underground space roofed by an elliptical, glazed vault, a groin with diameters of 78 and 60 meters that returns to the themes of the great elliptical coverings of sunken spaces, such as Pierre Vago's basilica at Lourdes (1958, diameters of 191 and 61 meters), Archigram's project for the Monaco Entertainments Center at Montecarlo (winners of the competition with Pierre Vago on the jury, 1969), Foster's American Air Museum at Duxford (1987-97) and, in its form and its quest for lightness and transparency, Frei Otto's City in the Arctic (1971). The story of the building is a complicated and dramatic one, but what is important is that, in Poitiers' project, the lightweight technology has been contaminated by its visceral contact with the ground, and that the vault, along with the external structures, is a great landmark, more in a conceptual and material sense than a visual one, rather than a mere demonstration of technological efficiency. The cosmogonic sense of the relationship between earth and sky, which is constructively turned on its head in the opposition between earthwork and roofwork, is underlined by the demonstrative clarity of the models and the rendered images, in which the relation between the chthonic world of the playing field and the great eye gazing at the sky embodies the deepest meaning of that architecture.

UTOPIAN, BRUT AND POST-HUMAN In his representation of the Sporthalle Poitiers deployed an exceptionally vast range of diverse and disquieting means of communication and expression. A personal experience: I remember when his materials arrived at our magazine, Lotus. Usually architects and designers send us a dozen color slides, five or six drawings in A4 format, a couple of pictures of the model and a page-long technical report, all tucked into a plastic envelope in turn enclosed in a nondescript DHL or FedEx package. But André sent us a gigantic box, a cardboard crate out of which spilled, as colorful and mysterious as Christmas presents, materials and publications that we had never seen, projects of which we knew almost nothing. And above all the materials of the Sporthalle, which were abundant and contradictory. The photographs showed a building that succeeded in being at once elegant and rugged, bringing together lightness and darkness. The technical drawings were perfectly balanced and highly professional, without affectations or illustrative concessions of any kind. But the photographs of the construction site, almost all of them taken at night, already added a powerful element of deliberate suggestion, with their sharp colors and scenic layout clearly inspired by a movie set. A scene in which you would expect, at any moment, the landing of the flying saucer and a close encounter of the third kind with extraterrestrial beings. Even the pictures of the model showed a surprising setting, a sort of post-atomic ruin in which the traces of a possible Apollonian order were violently infringed by the inertia of the raw metal. The rendering presented a landscape even more like a scene from a science-fiction movie, in which the athletes became glowing radioactive specters engaged in a game for which the prize was clearly some sort of ruthless punishment, some unspeakable violence. The absolutely real design of a constructed building had generated a disquieting jumble of simulacra of architecture and life, and was contaminated by alien presences that, like an invading army, cheerfully made camp in the ruins of a building whose function and meaning were no longer comprehensible. This fantastic proliferation of signals of ruin, of physical and moral decay, of catastrophe, perhaps conveyed the drama of an inner conflict, a surfacing of the unconscious that testified, through enigmas, to the splitting of the will in divergent directions.

BIOTECHNOLOGICAL, SEXUAL, AND IRREVERENT IMAGERY The direction courageously embarked on in the Sporthalle of Halstenbek was – let us hope only temporarily – abandoned in favor of a new organicist and futuristic line. Apparently this was a flight forward, an act of distancing from the reality of the concrete architecture to find new stimuli and new horizons.

The enigmatic building known as "The Fish" in Berlin and the X-1 highrise office block, Media City Port (Hamburg, 1996), represent an intermediate phase, in which the rigor of high-tech is softened in an imagery more biased towards symbolization and analogy with the world of organic forms. The elegant spindle-shaped profile is reminiscent of the mast of a sailboat, around which the floors of the various levels are wrapped with the grace of a sail filled with wind. The naval analogy is a recurrent theme of hightech – it would be impossible to imagine the stays, masts and shrouds of Foster, Piano and Rogers without the reference to sailing – and in the X-1 project this was taken to the level of figurative and symbolic hypertrophy, amidst references to highbrow culture – Constantin Brancusi's series of Birds – and a more naturalistic and Pop symbology, similar to the one used by Future Systems. Subsequently, Poitiers devoted himself to the staging of fantastic scenes animated by embryos, fragments of a history of the immediate future, prefigurations of an architecture that periodically seems to be on the point of coming into existence, but that is then, at least up to now, always leapfrogged by less utopian hypotheses, with deeper roots in the here and now of what is actually feasible.

PLUG-IN ARCHITECTURE In the projects he has worked on since 1997 Poitiers has abandoned his last ties with the world of Anglo-American high technology to set off decisively along the road of a plug-in architecture, i.e. an architecture that, like Archigram's Plug-In City, is set down on the ground like an extraneous and autonomous object, new, potentially mobile and repeatable and situationist. The Donut, the structure that was supposed to house the headquarters of the German Green party, is a political manifesto in its transparency and in its temporary and virtually reversible lightness. Set amidst the greenery of a park surrounded by the square blocks of Berlin, the Donut reacts against the dull stability of the nineteenth-century fabric. Its glass skin, its circular and homogeneous space and the softness of its continuously curving profile – a torus – prefigure a new, lighter and friendlier world. The Parish Center in Hamburg (1997) is set in the middle of a large triangular courtyard with the same concrete force, looking like a machine that is mysterious but reassuring in its streamlined profiles, but also like a cell, a blob whose outer skin is nothing more than a soft rind, an envelope that isolates and defines a portion of space. His subsequent projects have been studies experimenting with and varying the architectural possibilities of the environmental bubble, moving along the uneasy seam between science fact and space fiction. The Nemos House in Bonn (2000) is a spaceship that has landed in a metaphysical and silent piece of city, in which the most expressive element, as at the Parish Center, is the wood. The MM 18-21 building in Yokohama (2000) is a gleaming and mysterious solid located between the harbor and the city. The Kajen Restaurant in Hamburg (2001) is set on the arc of a circumference as if it were the station of a hypothetical accelerator of atomic particles. The Blip Building in Bonn (2001), located at the center of a large square with a traffic circle, does not belong to the urban fabric but to its infrastructure, to the road system, from which it springs like a luminous and troubling biotech bloom.

PLASMA, AUTOMATIC ARCHITECTURE The most recent goal on Poitiers' journey is Plasma, the liquid, organic and living material; a substance that is active and inert at the same time, liable to alter in relation to functional and environmental factors. Plasma is a home, or rather an idea of habitat, of livable space derived from the reworking on the computer of an industrially manufactured object. An object of design, in this case the container of the G-Shock watch is taken as the matrix of a process that, with the help of CAD software, can develop endless variants in relation to needs of space, structure, materials, modes of assembly of the basic cell, etc. The result is a generator of architectural form, a system of production that can be multiplied in endless practices and applications in accordance with a technical objectivity, and a principle of pure functionality; a method that, within a defined frame of operation, produces architecture in an automatic way.

The procedure used by Poitiers mixes different techniques and tactics, dipping into the reservoir of the avant-garde. Marcel Duchamp's readymades, the automatic writing of Raymond Roussel as taken up by André Breton and the celibate machines of Michel Carrouge stand in the background of an extreme experiment that, respecting the rules of the avant-garde, declares itself to be purely technical, that "its construction is in linc with the concept 'form follows function'."

Once again Poitiers addresses the present and in the same moment leapfrogs it, shoots past it and produces figures and scenarios for the future. The project is presented as the fruit of a disenchanted and productive attitude, as the outcome of an acceptance of the world of industrial production, of merchandise and consumption. Fortunately, Plasma is evidently a critical operation as well, an action that, in the spirit of "Dada", flouts the scale of established values and assigns new ones. The electronic – neo-mechanistic – determinism embodied by CAD software interprets the will of the operator and imposes its own rules, it seizes hold of objects in order to grind them up and then spit them out stripped of their original meaning. The "aesthetics of expendability" is nullified, brought back within an artistic process that is itself bound by a logic of performance. The objective is the attainment of an idea, an image, a complex way of thinking which does not take as its sole reference the industrial policy of a company and its marketing service, unlike what happens in industrial design: the production of the object is not seen as a unique and ultimate goal, but as a stage in the development of an original vision of architecture and a means of verifying it.

PROJEC

TS

205-01

HALSTENBEK / 1993

SPORTS HALL

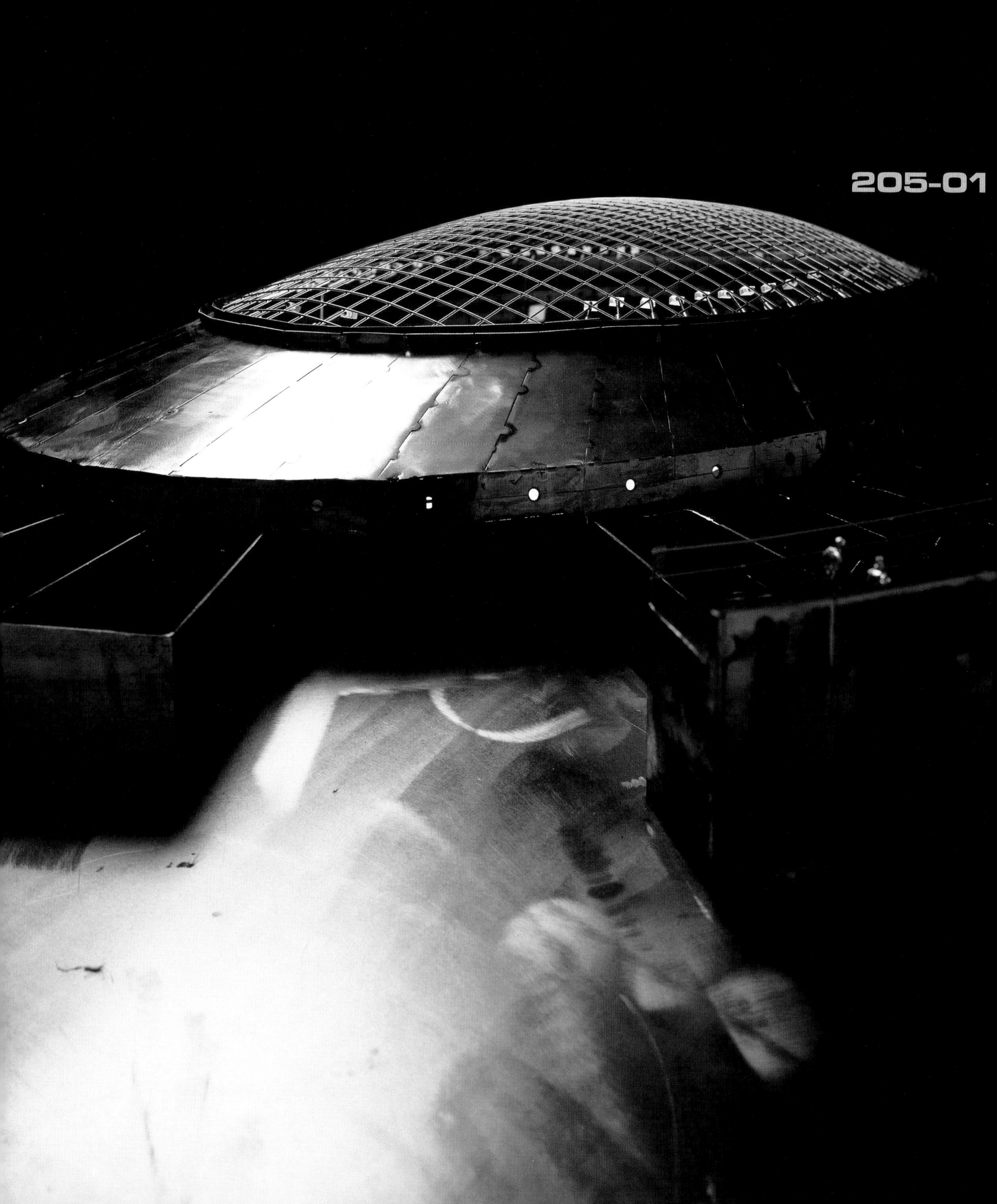

205-01

An extroverted intimacy fills this light volume, which is contained by a wall of exposed concrete, so that your eyes are constantly directed upwards to the outside world above the horizon, while your body remains protected inside the building's excavated ground.

BURIED ALIEN

There is no sign of the building until the last minute, nothing to suggest that it is there at all until you reach the clearing between the town hall and the residential area. A glass dome arches out of the fields, shallow as the back of a tortoise. By the road is a transparent lift that could lead to an underground car park, and next to it flights of steps curving down under the ground. At the end of this, a glass door leads to underground casemates in exposed concrete, lit sparsely but effectively. Corridors disappear into the depths of the space, curling softly round the corner. As you try to find your way, you intuitively follow the light, which paradoxically seems to get brighter the deeper under the ground you are. Then finally there is another glass door, and you're back in the world in a flash; the sky soars above your head, even though you are still a floor below the horizon. Instead of a normal ceiling, the sports hall is covered by a glazed roof tent. Light is the only thing that comes down from the world above the horizon, the noise stays outside. An extroverted intimacy fills this light volume, which is contained by an exposed concrete wall, so that your eyes are constantly directed upwards to the outside. The tops of the neighbouring trees and buildings are visible at the edge of the celestial eye, surrounding the action in the sports hall with a peripheral trace of context – in complete contrast with the sense of clenched detachment that normally characterizes the interior atmosphere of sports halls. The fact that the building is buried has a positive effect above ground level as well, because its large volume can be integrated into the intricate neighbourhood in this way without dominating it. The sunken building eliminates problems like deep shadows and the noise made by its users, all of which would have had to be faced if the same volume had been placed on the grass like a box.

Although it is integrated into the context, the building maintains an alien quality that is all the more effective because the spatial origin of this intrusion cannot be located directly. Ultimately a large part of the building volume that is above the ground remains invisible as well, because the periphery of the elliptical truncated cone is planted with greenery. At the top, the camouflage of the artificial mound suddenly shifts into the transparent effect of the enormous glass dome, a suspended glass canopy construction curved on two axes, with an area of a good 1000 square metres, which makes artificial light entirely superfluous during the day. To keep heat transfer within ecologically tolerable limits, the dome is glazed in solar insulating glass with laminated safety glass on the underside. Below that is a horizontal sunshade that can be extended when needed and is otherwise kept folded away at the side. The low-energy, reinforced concrete hall is sunk four metres into the ground, and takes advantage of the constant soil temperature of approx. 10 degrees for self-cooling and self-heating, (which considerably reduces winter fuel consumption in comparison with a standard hall). In winter the hall is heated by an air heating system set in the concrete wall above the point at which it bends inwards. 100 powerful nozzles set in the wall fill the space with pre-heated air, which moves along the inner concrete shell to the peak of the suspended glass dome by the Coanda effect, and from there it is forced down to the floor and sucked in again under the stand structure to be reconditioned – thus the air in the building is on a closed circuit. But phenomenologically the room literally seems to reach for the sky – a fairly astonishing use of space given that the maximum height of the dome is only 12.65 metres.

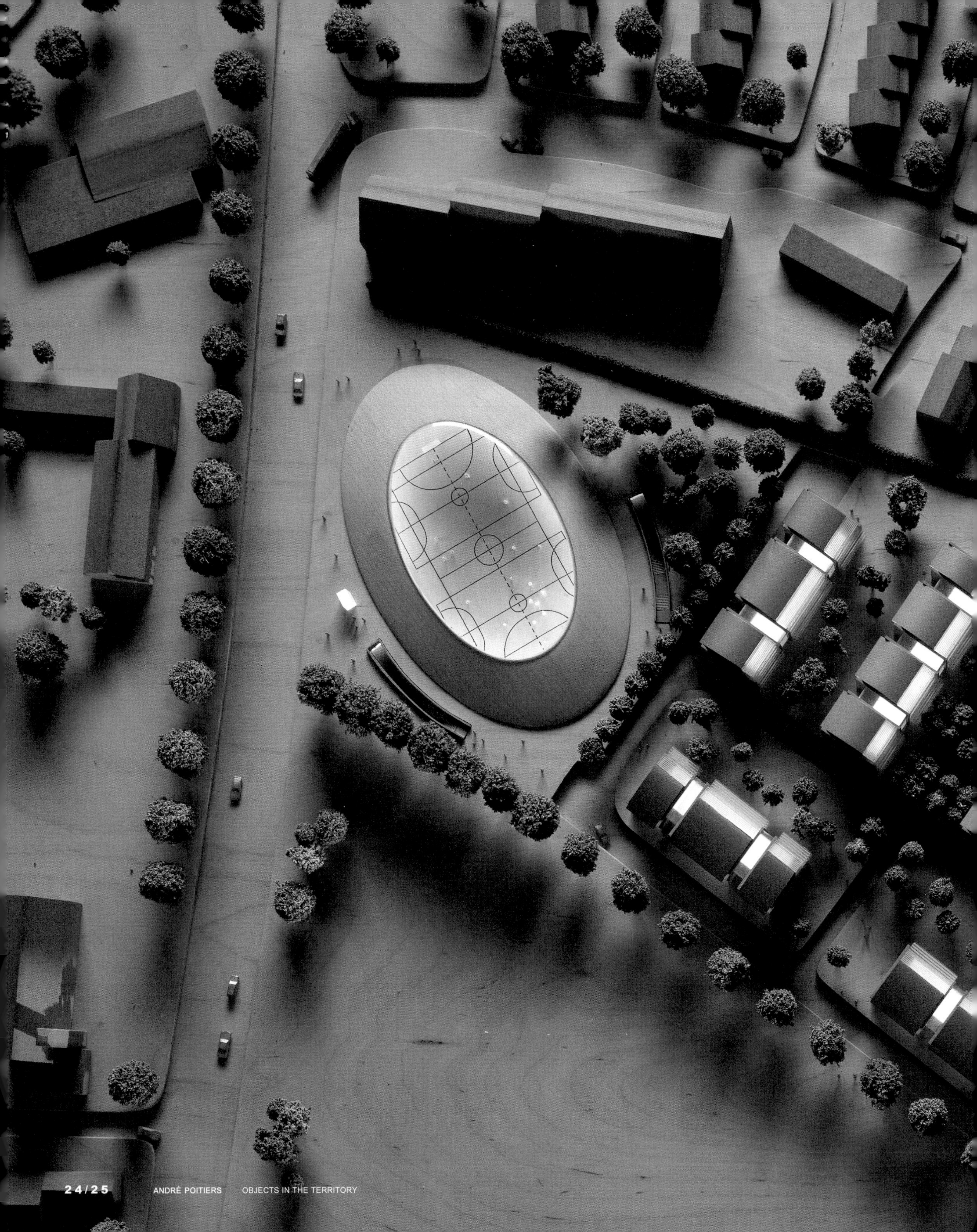

MASTER PLAN FOR THE DEVELOPMENT OF THE LÜDEMANN PLOT,
SPORTS HALL, 104 RESIDENTIAL UNITS, MODEL PHOTOGRAPH

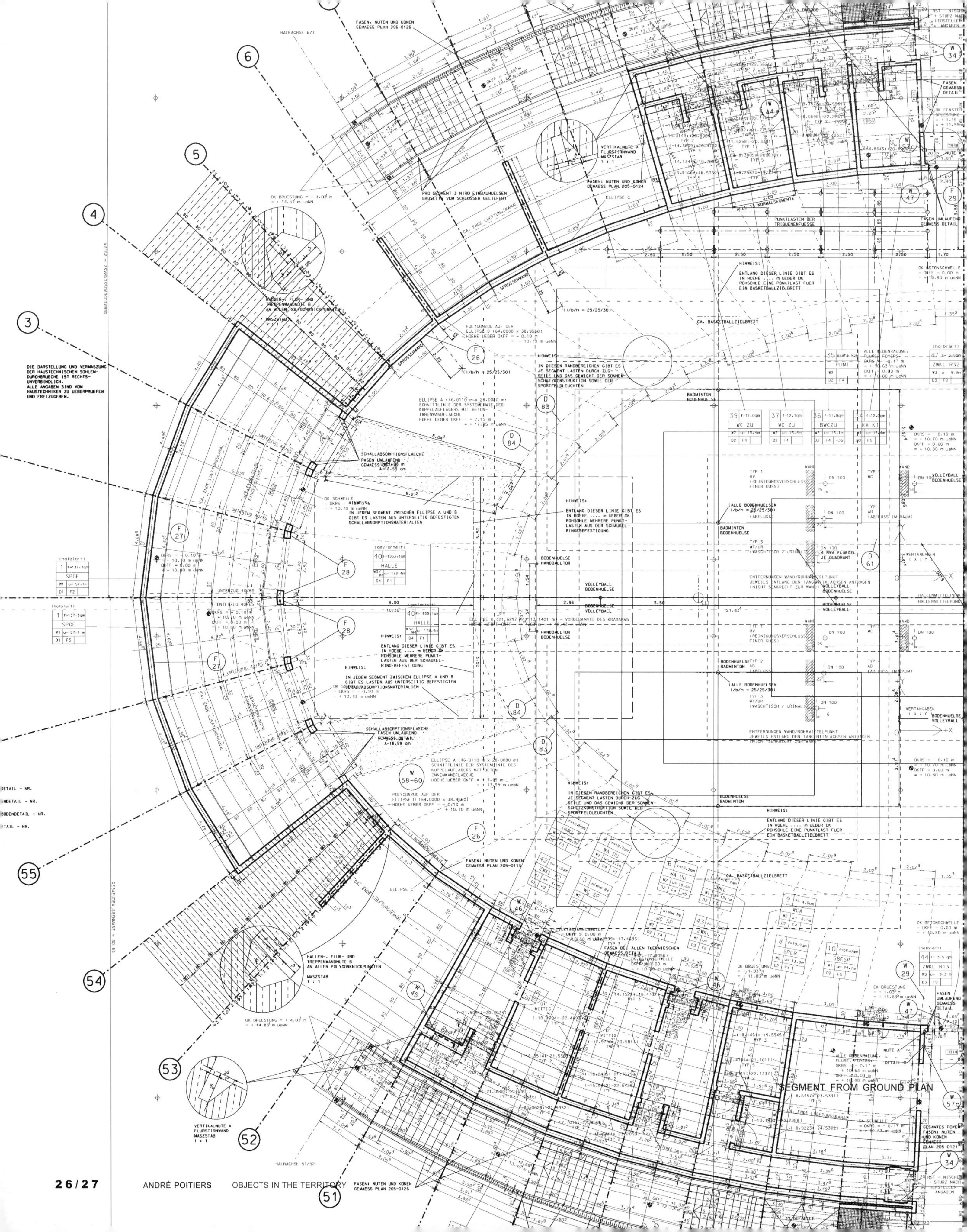

SEGMENT FROM GROUND PLAN

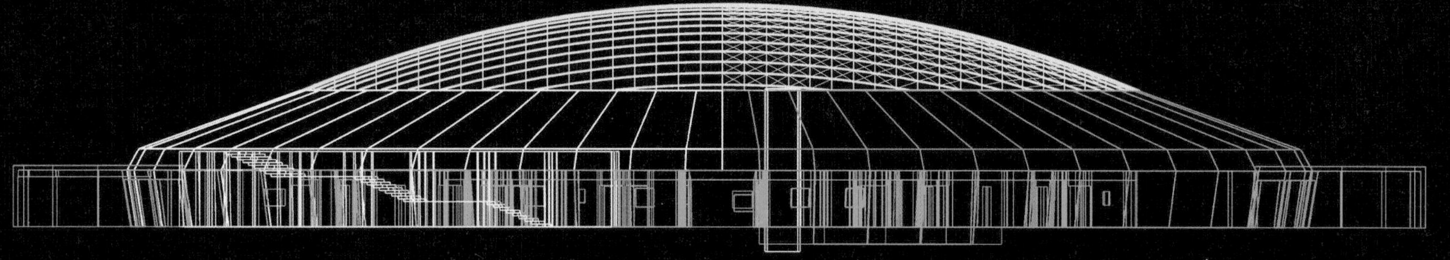

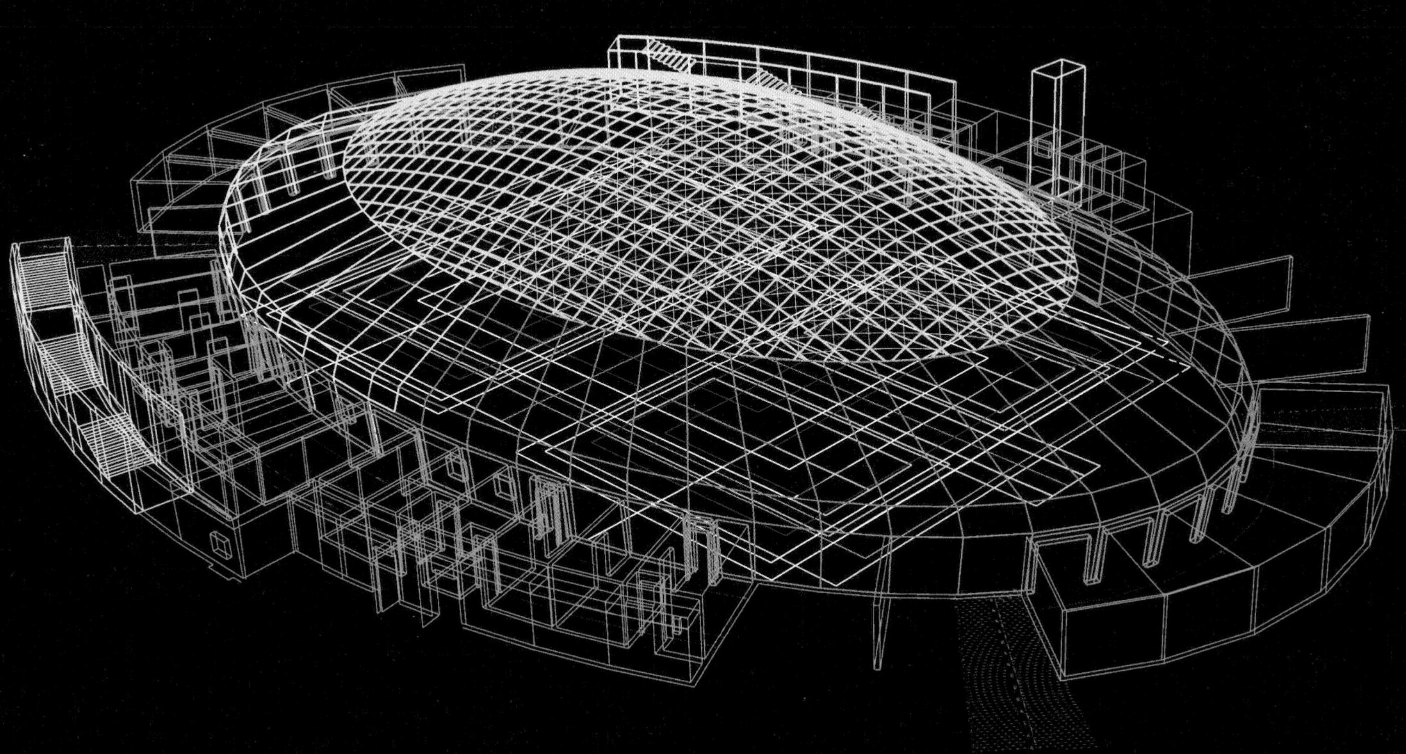

3D MODEL OF THE BUILDING

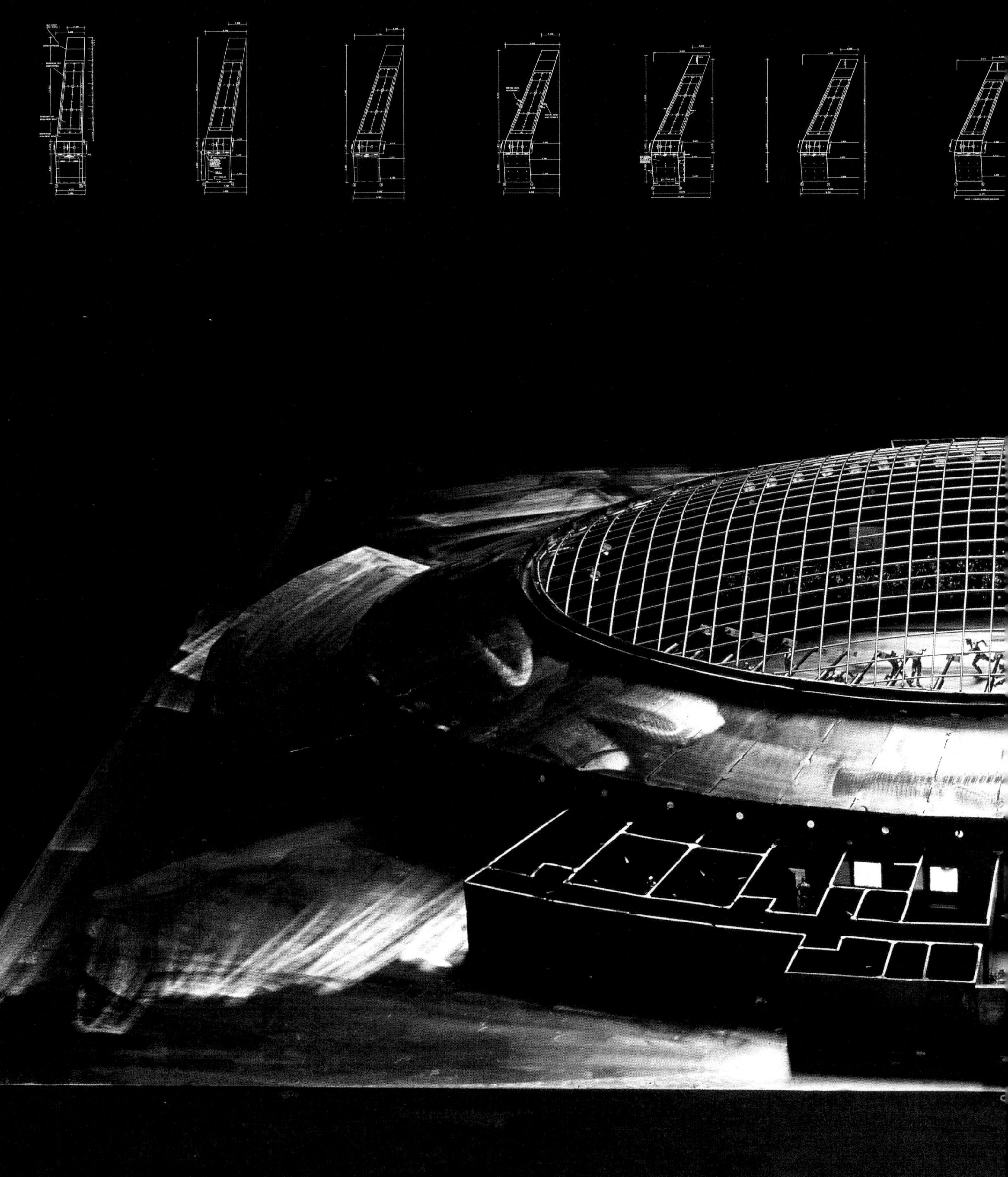

STEEL MODEL OF THE SPORTS HALL
DEVELOPED VIEW OF THE CONCRETE SHUTTERING

205-01

205-01

205-01

INTERIOR VIEW OF THE SPORTS HALL

AERIAL PHOTOGRAPH OF THE COMPLETED SPORTS HALL

349-02

OFFICE BUILDING / HAMBURG / 1996

X1

349-02

The X1 Tower deploys a cloning operation using Brancusi's "Bird" as its genetic material. Blowing the volume of the sculpture up into breathtaking dimensions, the building heralds the ground-breaking transformation the harbour is going to face in the very near future.

ART CLONING

Like other modern ports, Hamburg harbour is nomadic territory that has moved further and further out of town in recent decades. But unlike Rotterdam, it has never abandoned the town completely, and is still a major urban player. Even the infrastructural landscape of the new container terminal is not in some no man's land outside the city gates, but near the centre on the south bank of the Elbe in Waltershof, a genuine spectacle much enjoyed from the other side of the river.

For this reason, the development of the central, historic inner harbour is crucially important for Hamburg's future identity. A key feature here is the Speicherstadt area, a dense complex of warehouse buildings that is hardly used for port-related work now because loading and unloading methods have changed completely. This development shows most clearly in the "Hafen-City", a major urban development project for converting the old Speicherstadt into a residential and service complex. The boundary of Hamburg's free port has been shifted east to accommodate the plan. This involves a not insignificant redefinition of territory: hitherto the Speicherstadt, as part of the free port, had been a customs-free area: no customs duty was levied on goods that were turned round here. Shifting the boundary means that the Speicherstadt is now part of the city. The X1 project is sited on the foremost tip of the Dalmannkai, and marks this transformation most strikingly. As Hamburg has very few high-rise buildings, a tower seemed the ideal way to attract attention to the location and signal the change it has undergone. The urban development plan aims to change the use of the area rather than its form, but the X1 project interprets the emerging development as a radical redefinition of the whole situation. The project is also acting out the whole process of change in its own right, by transforming the typology of the high-rise. It is using a cloning strategy to escape from the monoculture of vertically extruded cuboids and cylinders. Here Poitiers uses Brancusi's sculpture "Bird" as genetic material: its volume is blown up to the scale of the new tower, without any detours or compromises. The load-bearing structure of the building is an eccentrically placed core, with the floor plates suspended on traction cables. Following the fluid shape of Brancusi's sculpture, each storey has a different floor area.

The project imitates the stepped base of the sculpture by extruding the whole plot slightly. The core of the building is stuck into this plinth like a pin; the plinth houses the lobby and all the access systems. This level rises towards the town, and the height differential created at the quay is filled with a glass façade, thus creating a visual link between the lobby and the city. As the roof of the sloping plane is planted with trees, the footprint of the tower does not appear any larger than the point at which the pin is stuck in. This seems to negate one of the fundamental statical laws of architecture, which states that a building can only get narrower towards the top because of the principles of load bearing. This bird squeezes itself in at the bottom, and waits until it is in the air to spread its wings.

349-02

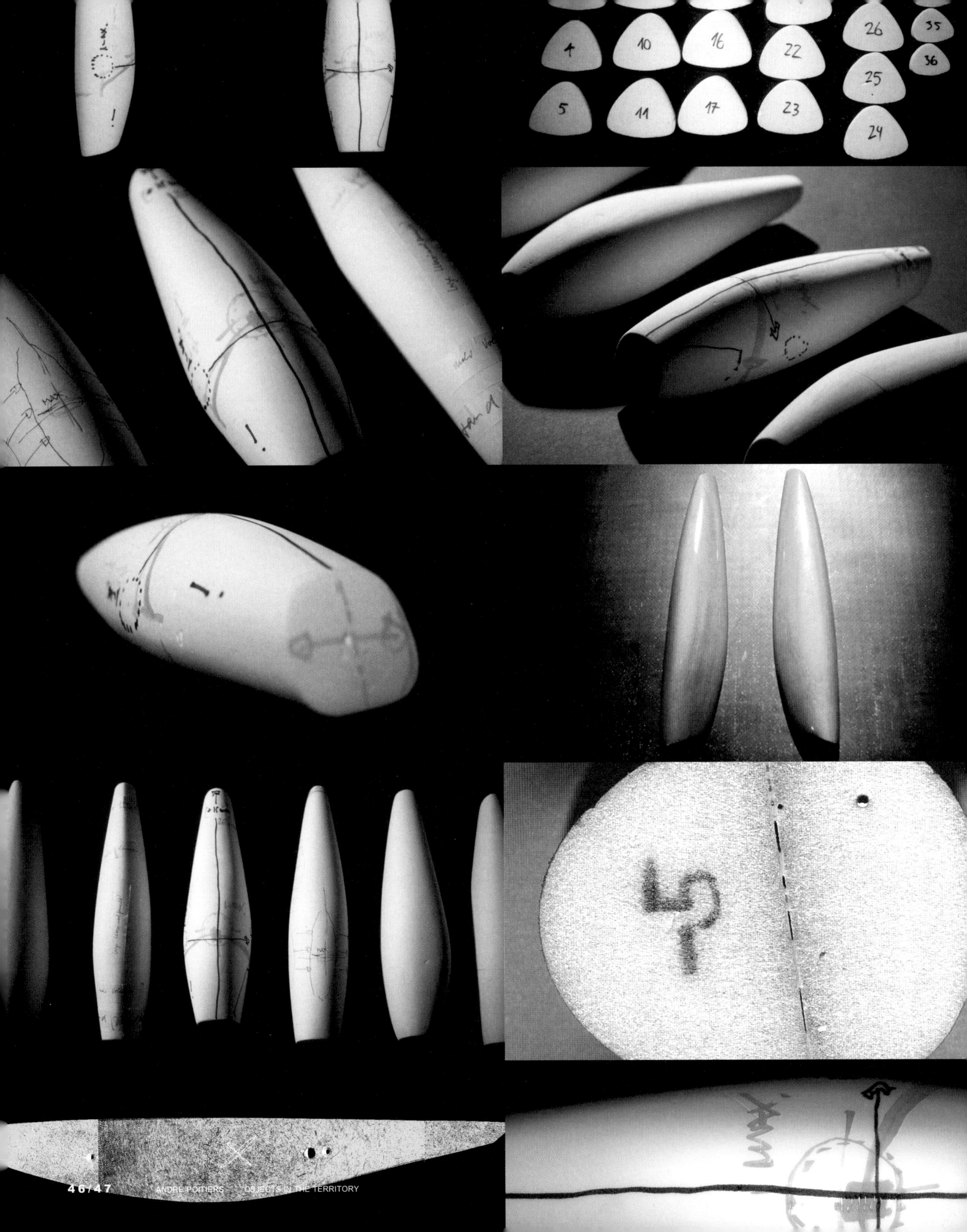
4
10
16
22
26
35
36
25
5
11
17
23
24
5

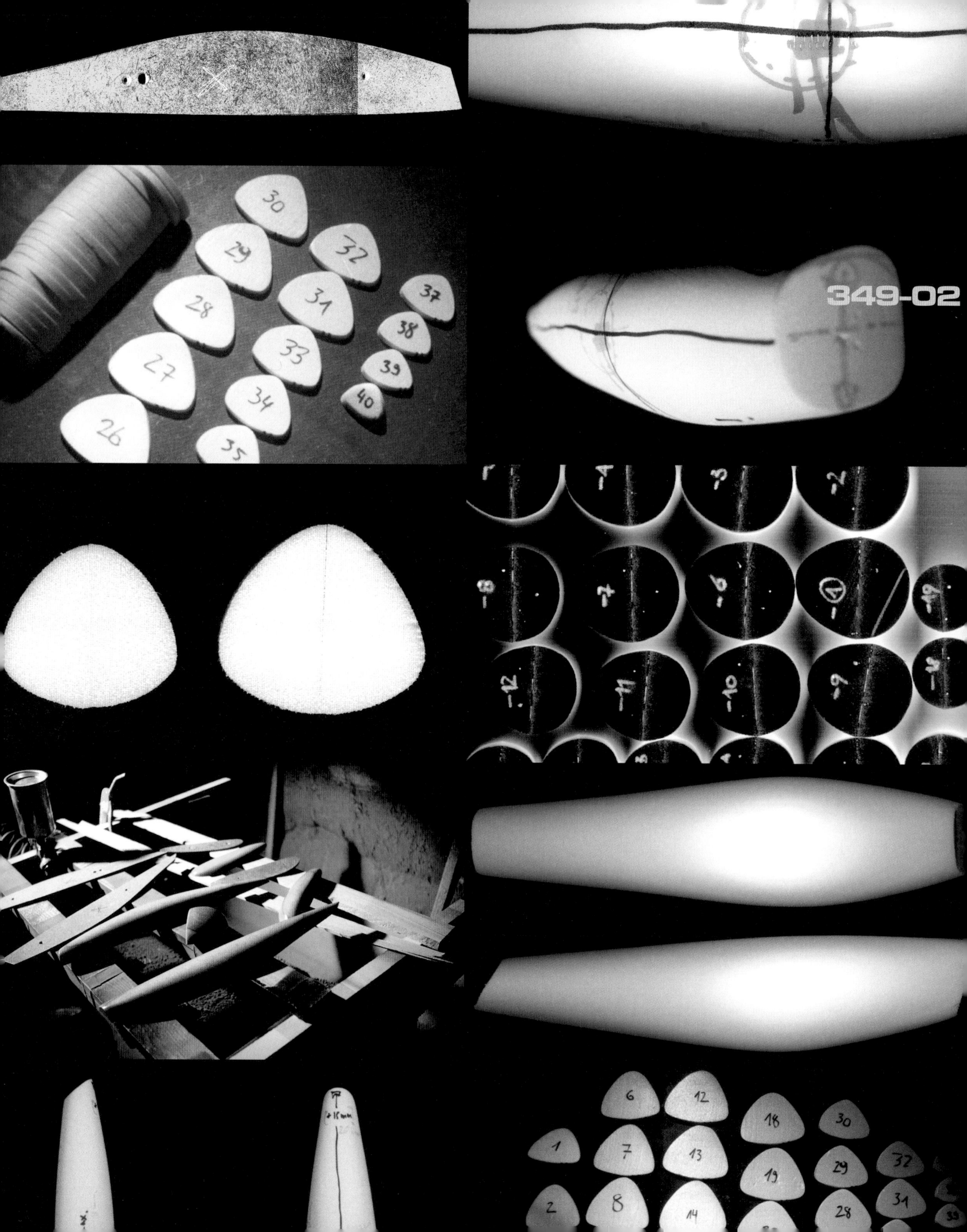
349-02

349-02

URBAN CONTEXT, DALMANNKAI, HAMBURG, MODEL PHOTOGRAPH

248-03

OFFICE BUILDING / BERLIN / 1997

DONUT

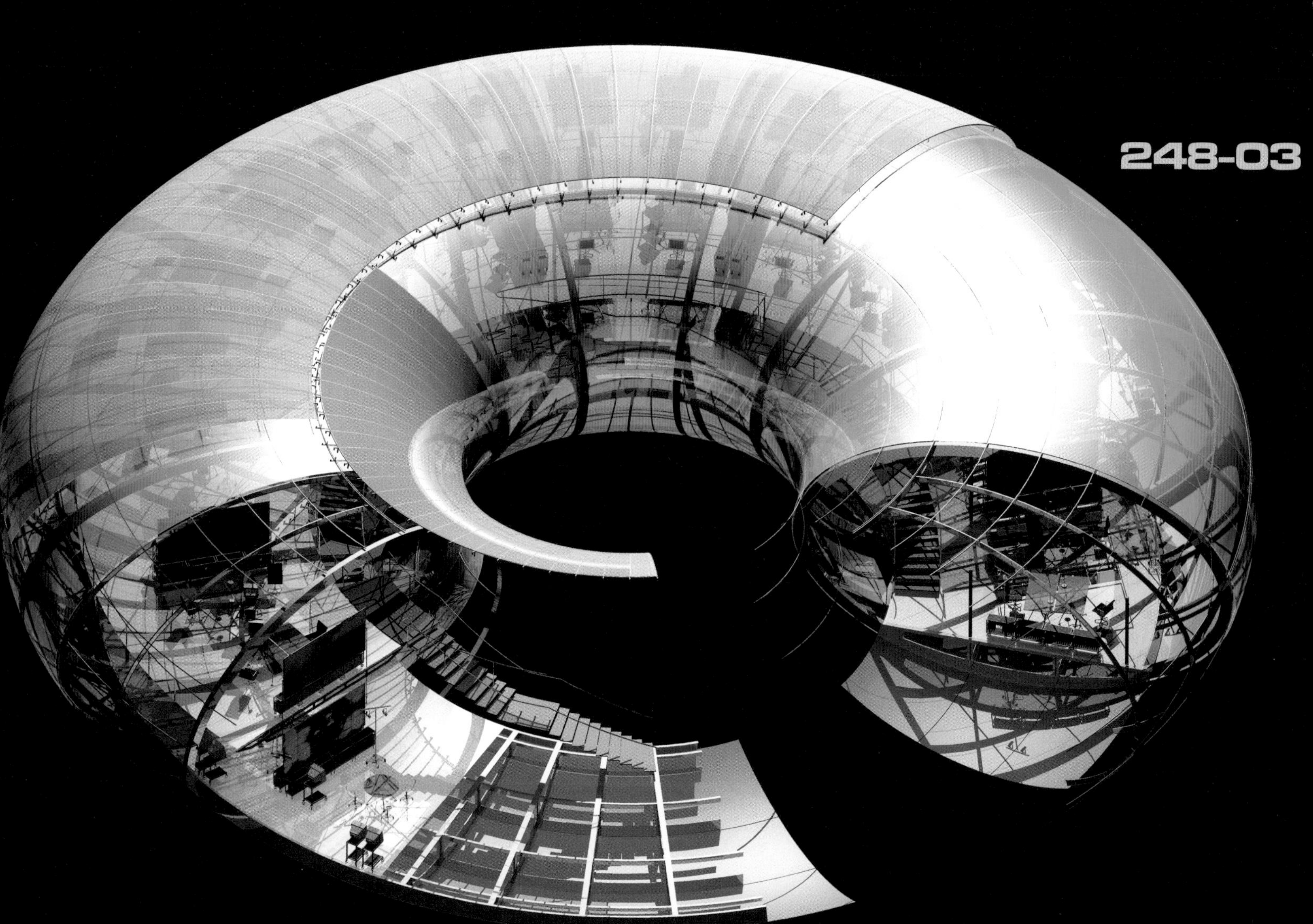

248-03

By avoiding so-called "natural materials" like wood, clay or planted roofs the building unambiguously resists any folksy interpretation of Ecological Architecture, searching instead for an eco-logic of architecture, in which nature and culture no longer contrast with, but complement each other.

BUILDING POLITICS

Shortly before the Germany parliamentary elections in 1998, the Hamburg "ZEIT Magazin" invited four architects to design a new party headquarters for the four political parties represented in the German parliament. Poitiers Architects drew the lot for the Green Party. The architects were free to choose their own site. The project they produced is presented appropriately site-less: provisionally placed in a Berlin block structure, it looks as much out of place as the Green Party did when making their historical entrance into the Bundestag in 1980. Just as the party's elected representatives mixed deliberate provocations like sneakers and pullovers into Germany's tried-and-tested political culture, Poitiers' building refuses to submit to the rules of the game dictated by the context. It stands on its site as though just parked there for the time being, as though it does not want to pin itself down to a particular place. The bridge that emerges hesitantly to offer access to the outside world makes it clear that we are entering a different world here.

The party headquarters is nothing like a fortress for bigwigs: the interior is more like a research laboratory. The work-stations are separated by projection screens with images of environmental disasters, climate damage and eco-scandals, permanently reminding those working here of their political duties. All the furniture is on castors, so that the space can be arranged as flexibly as possible. Also the rotation principle turns up again in the spatial concept for this building – originally devised by the Greens as an administrative preventive measure against congealing political power – as the diagram of the roller-blade wheel makes clear. As is well known, rotation keeps the centre free; centrifugal force keeps everything away from it. The higher the performance of the system, the greater the trend to the extremities of the volume. The principle of permanent re-orientation also determines the architecture's relationship with external influences. Thus the external sun-screens, divided into two segments for the inner and outer sections of the torus, are fixed to the façade so that they can move, and can thus respond to the current position of the sun. The building is heat-insulated by intelligent glass, whose permeability to heat and light can be regulated. Structurally the building consists of 16 identical steel torus segments, which can be pre-fabricated at reasonable cost, and assembled on site. The clear rejection of so-called "natural materials" like wood, clay or planted roofs unambiguously resists any folksy interpretation of Ecological Building – which is of course quite popular in the Greens' political set-up. In fact the project is looking for an eco-logic of architecture, in which nature and culture no longer contrast with, but complement each other. A consensus of this kind has still to be reached by the Green Party.

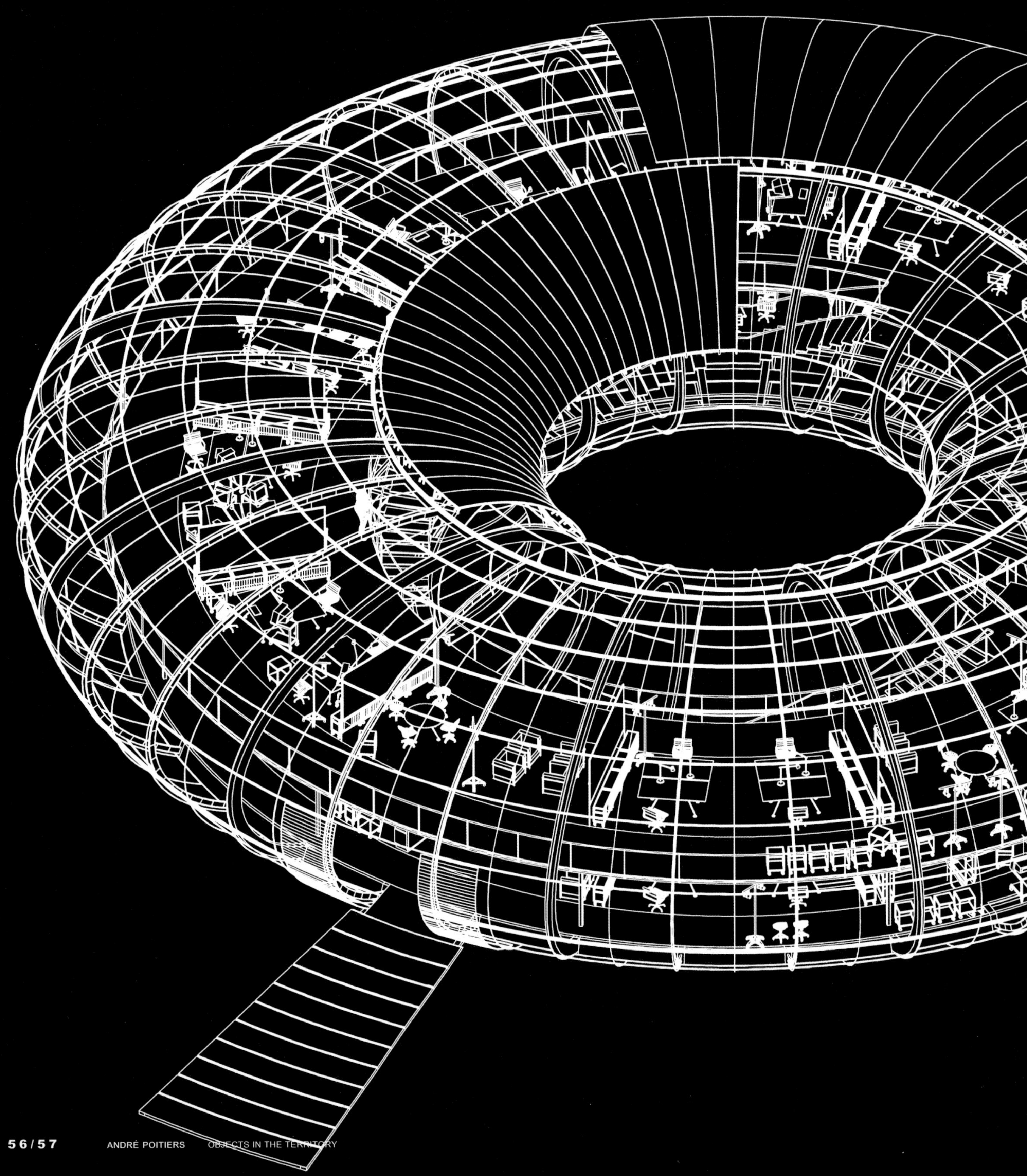

248-03

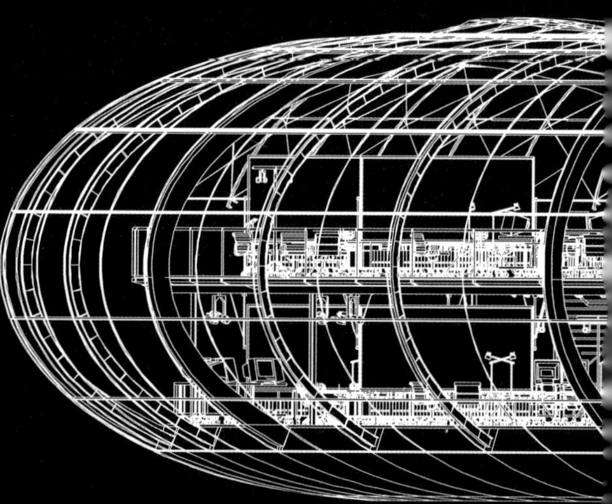

ISOMETRIC AND SIDE ELEVATION OF THE BUILDING

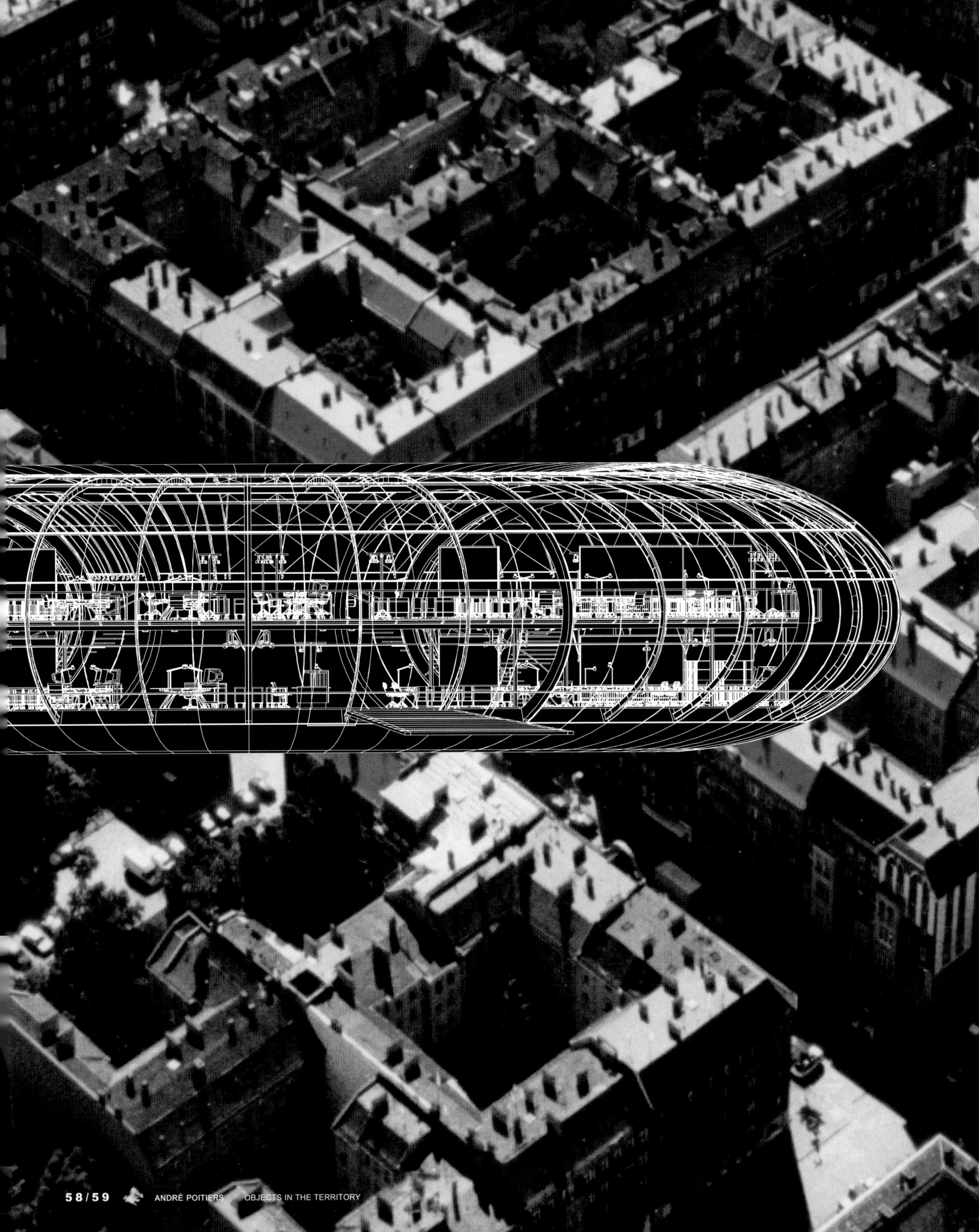

248-93

AERIAL PHOTOGRAPH OF PRENZLAUER BERG, PHOTO-MONTAGE WITH BUILDING

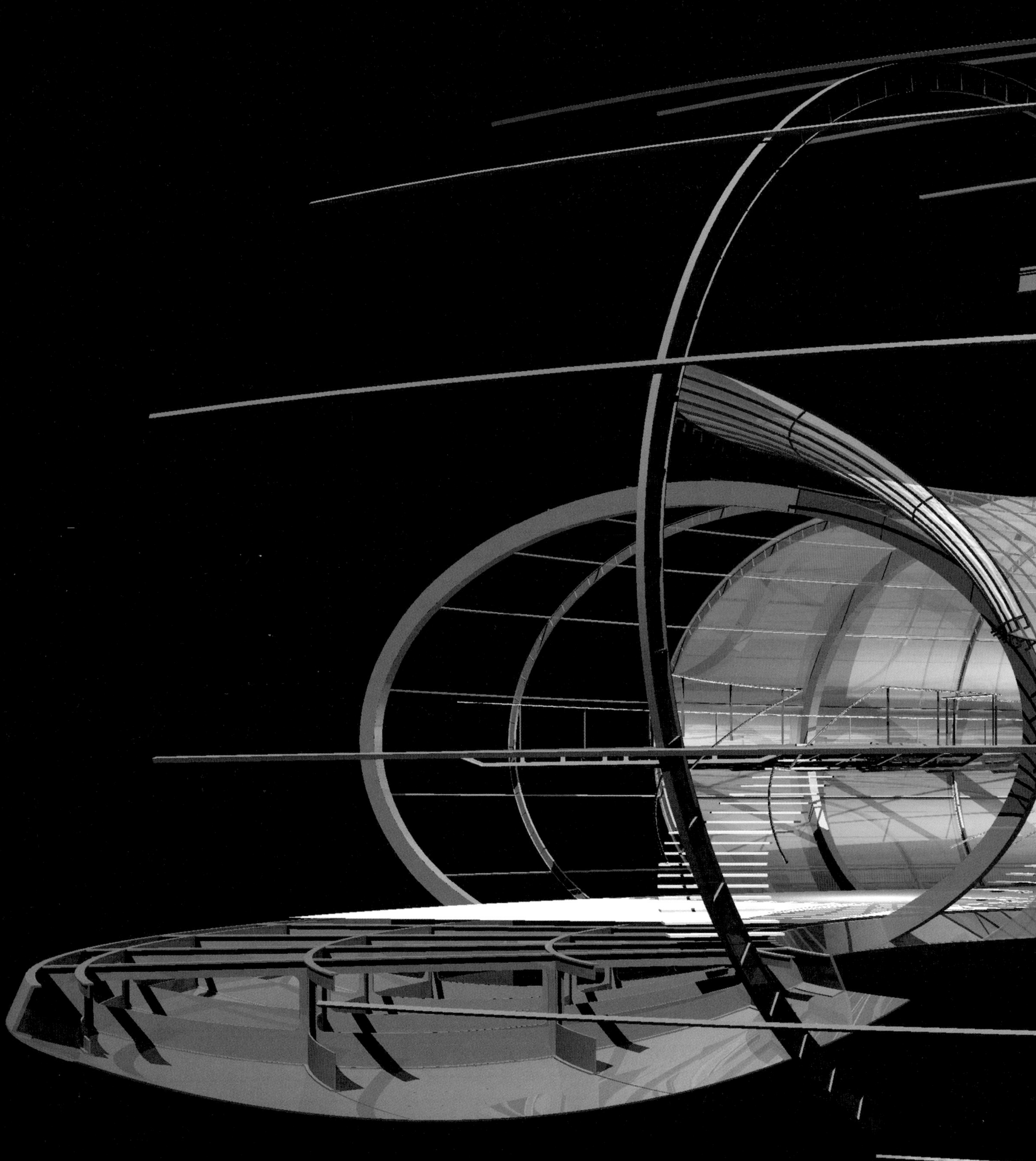

248-03

248-03

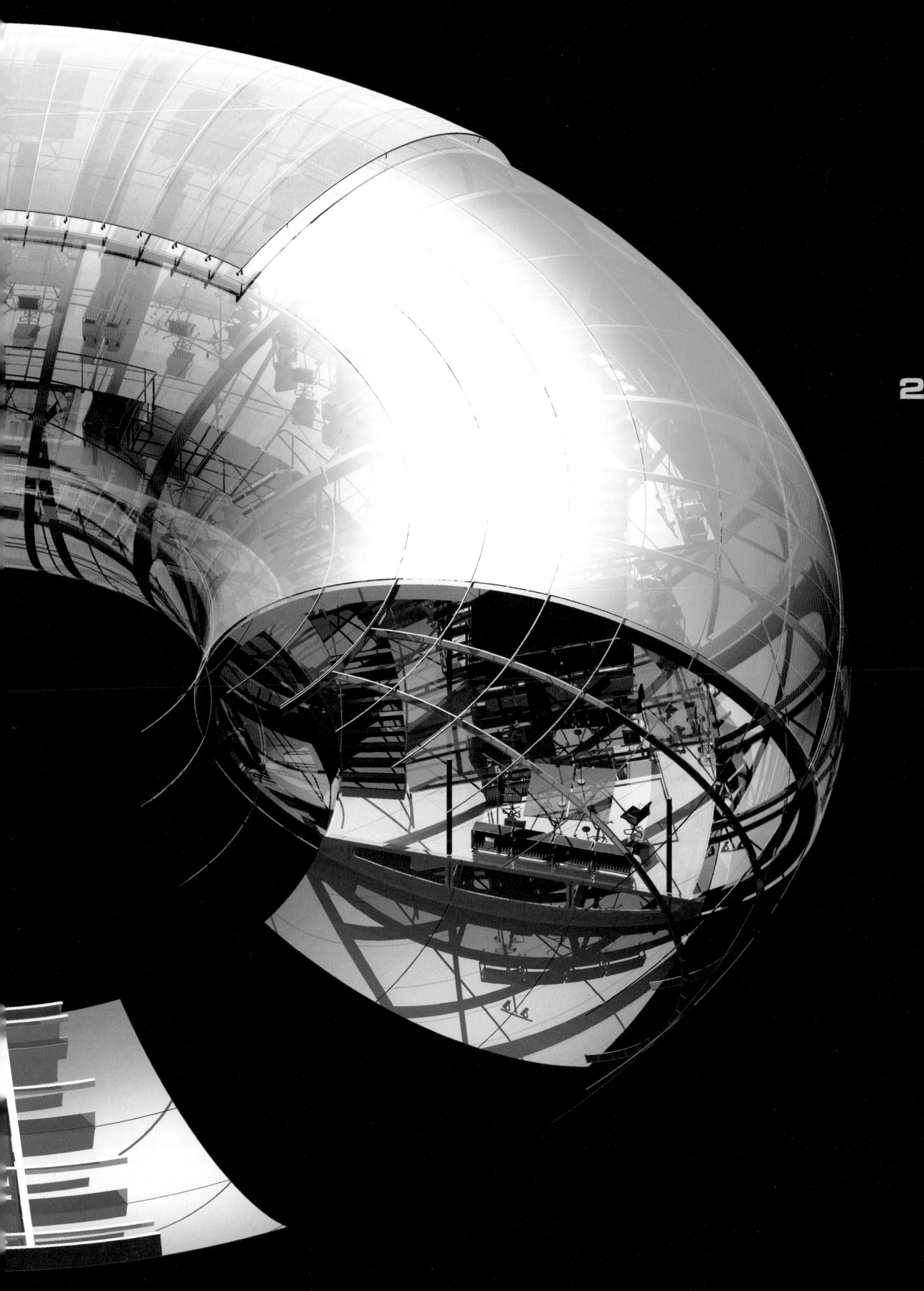

248-03

238-04

JOHNSALLEE / HAMBURG / 1997

PARISH CENTRE

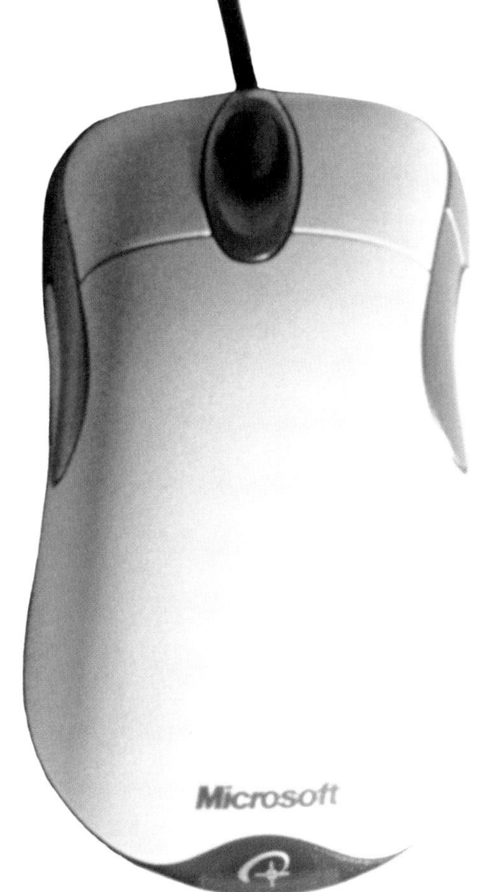

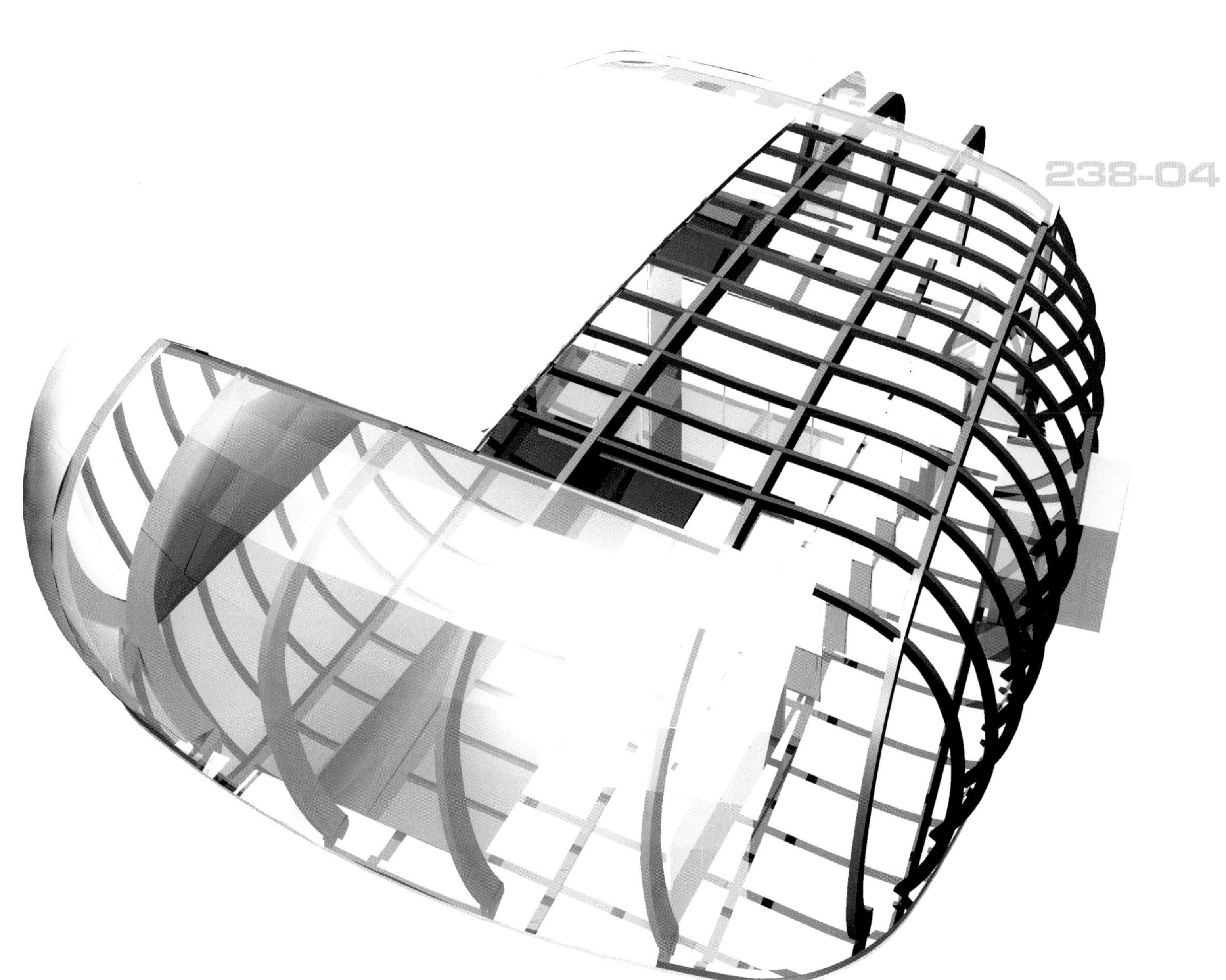
238-04

With all its corners washed away, the building sits inside the block like an erratic boulder; an appearance so archaic that it suggests some relic of times long past, and thus makes its surroundings, which seem historical today, look relatively recent.

HIDDEN ARK

The Johanneskirche in Hamburg decided to create a location outside the church building for its parish life, and so announced an architectural competition for a parish centre. But as the site slots tightly into the row of buildings on the perimeter of a block, there was no room for possible extensions. And so they decided to convert the neighbouring old building to accommodate the smaller elements of the building programme (kindergarten, parish rooms and dwellings), but to erect a new building inside the block for the large events hall.

The Poitiers Architects project uses this separation of the programme as the basis for an architectural and contextual strategy in which old and new buildings play completely different roles. The old building is interpreted as such: the architecture of the turn-of-the-century villa is interfered with as little as possible, and no attempt is made to suggest that the building is not part of the block. But then the new building stands out from its surroundings completely. It is reached from the old building by a walkway, and sits inside the block like an erratic boulder, apparently so archaic that it suggests some relic of times long past, and thus makes its surroundings, which seem historical today, look relatively recent. It is placed freely, and with its rounded volume is like an ark that has been taken out of the fabric of the city and is seeking a haven in the sunken garden world of the block interior. Placing the events hall outside heightens the sense of detachment from the surroundings hinted at by the church building's architectural introversion, eventually leading to a deterritorialization of the whole place. On the way from the church to the events room you are aware of the block space only for the short moment that you spend in the glazed passage between the two buildings. As soon as you reach the events hall you are in a different world, a place where the community can meet for everyday purposes in a self-chosen atmosphere of being shut away from the outside world. The ground plan consists essentially of a laterally inserted box with sanitary facilities, a small kitchen and chair store. This separates the events room from the meeting room, which is used as a back-stage area for theatre productions. Otherwise there are no fixed walls. The division between the hall and the foyer consists only of a folding screen that can disappear completely into a niche when necessary, so that the foyer area can be filled with chairs as 238-04
well. Given that room divisions which make sense for certain programmes are only there for as long as they are needed, the continuous curve of the hall is potentially always perceptible in its entirety.

This interior flexibility contrasts clearly with the monolithic weight of the exterior shape of the building, which seems as robust and protective as a ship's hull. The load-bearing structure is made up of curved glued timber trusses, clad on the inside with birch plywood. The outside of the building is covered with copper strips, and at night it is transformed into a darkly shimmering colossus by the lights from the dwellings around it. A wrapped interior that is alien in any outdoor space and thus at home everywhere.

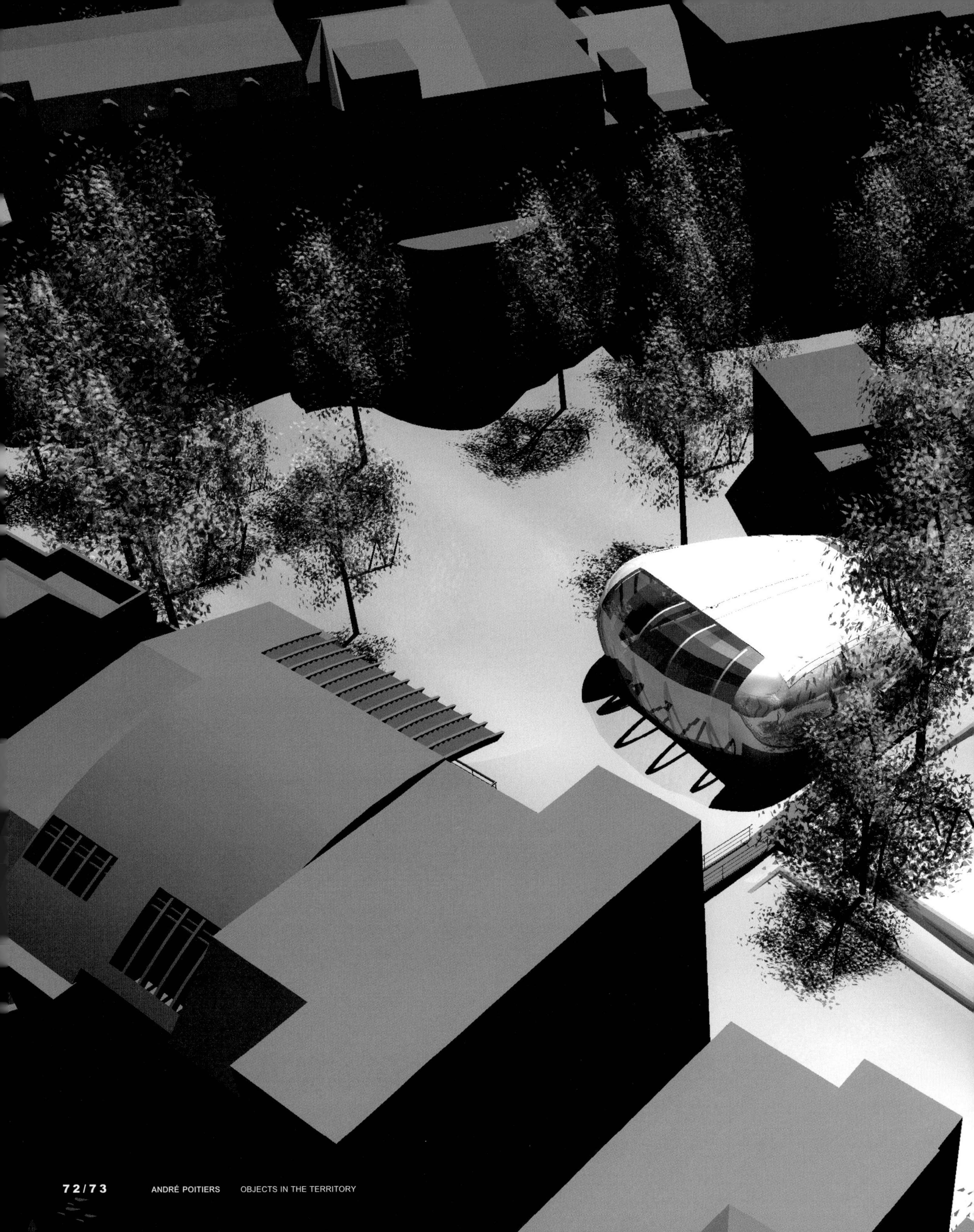

238-04
URBAN CONTEXT

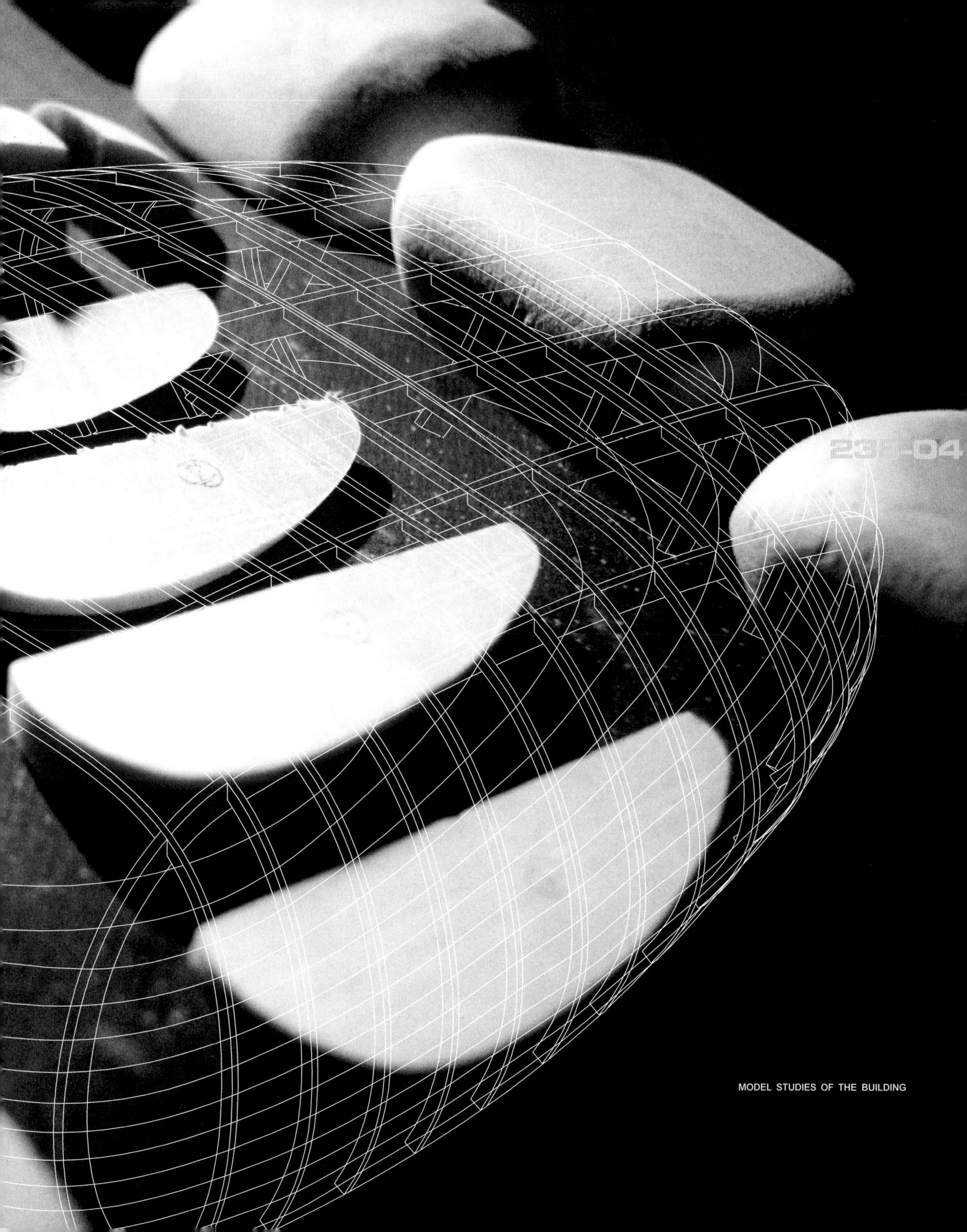

MODEL STUDIES OF THE BUILDING

238-04

MODEL PHOTOGRAPH WITH GROUND PLAN

702-05

1997

PLASMA HOUSE

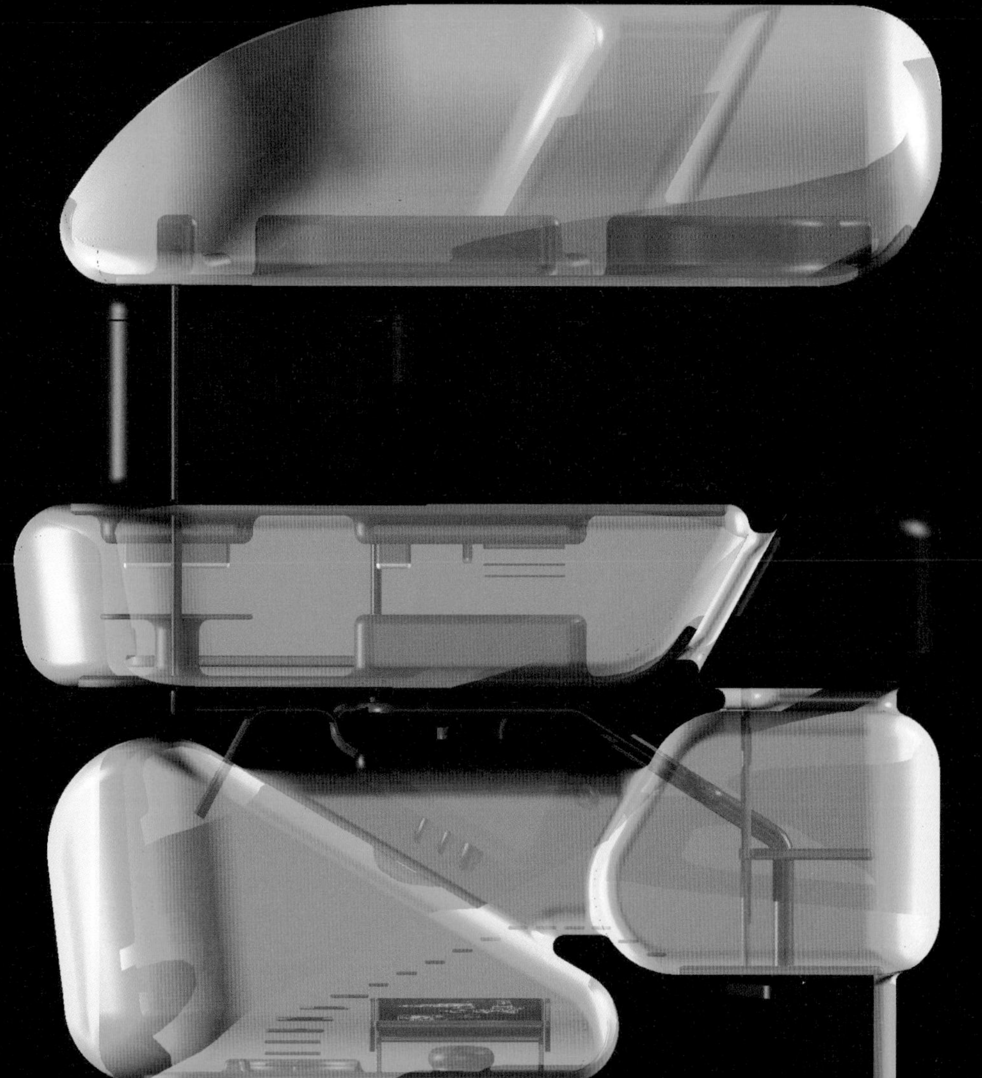

702-05

Combining Archigram's plug-in as an all-embracing system with Yona Friedman's megastructures as linking logistics, the Plasma House continues the sixties tradition of visionary architecture, but not without twisting the glorified aura of Utopia into a feasible endea-vour by today’s society.

LIVING IN (OUTER) SPACE

The Plasma House is a project without a site, a client or a commission, but it presents an ambitious conceptual agenda. The starting point is a re-examination of the module, both in architectural and urban terms. In the Plasma House, the module features a radical separation of the envelope and the internal form. This is a concept that Poitiers has borrowed from a contemporary design product: the G-Shock Watch. The special feature of this watch lies in the fact that it is offered with packaging that does not house the watch just temporarily: packaging and watch make up an integral system. The case is always the same, but the watch inside can vary between twenty different types. The type that is used can always be identified directly from the outside, because the casing is completely transparent. The case represents the maximum possible space for the interior. It cannot go beyond the case, but can develop unhindered within its volume.

This dialectic between inside and outside turns up again in the Plasma House, which fills the design prototype of the G-Shock Watch with the programme of a single-family house. The first step in this metamorphosis is the definition in terms of scale, derived in this case from a predetermined urban height limit. This Maximum Envelope forms the starting point for the design of the house, which is thus planned from the outside inwards. The typical room depths and ceiling heights defined by functions produce the fundamental spatial structure and possible division of volume. In a sophisticated process of optimization, which can be seen as a kind of fine tuning, the volumes are adapted to their functions stage by stage – e.g. by eliminating unnecessary parts of the volume and creating meaningful hierarchies. Once the basic volumetric form is established, the individual components are linked structurally (in terms of equipment and access) and also defined in terms of their visual permeability (transparency/opacity). Finally the structure produced is placed in the outer envelope that started the process off, as a building within a building.

This envelope completely shuts the house off from its physical context. And so for Poitiers it could also be "standing" in space. In fact the logistics of the building are reminiscent of the techno-Futurism of Science Fiction architecture. For example, movement between the levels of the house is on vertical lifting platforms. What first seems like a capricious cliché turns out to be the detail of an urban design concept continued in the building. The house is entered from below, also via a lifting platform in a socket system that docks the house with an infrastructural network of underground connecting pipes – together with countless other buildings that, following the model of the G-Shock Watch, could house a whole range of functions and also follow the principle of "Function follows Form". Beyond its nominal typology the Plasma House is thus defined as a variable module for metabolistic urbanism. Combining Archigram's plug-in as an all-embracing system with Yona Friedman's megastructures as linking logistics, Poitiers is quite obviously continuing the sixties' tradition of visionary architecture with – but under the changed condition of – the current situation. Hence in Poitiers' version the definitively Utopian character of that architecture gives way to the assertion of its feasibility, which is supported by current technical development.

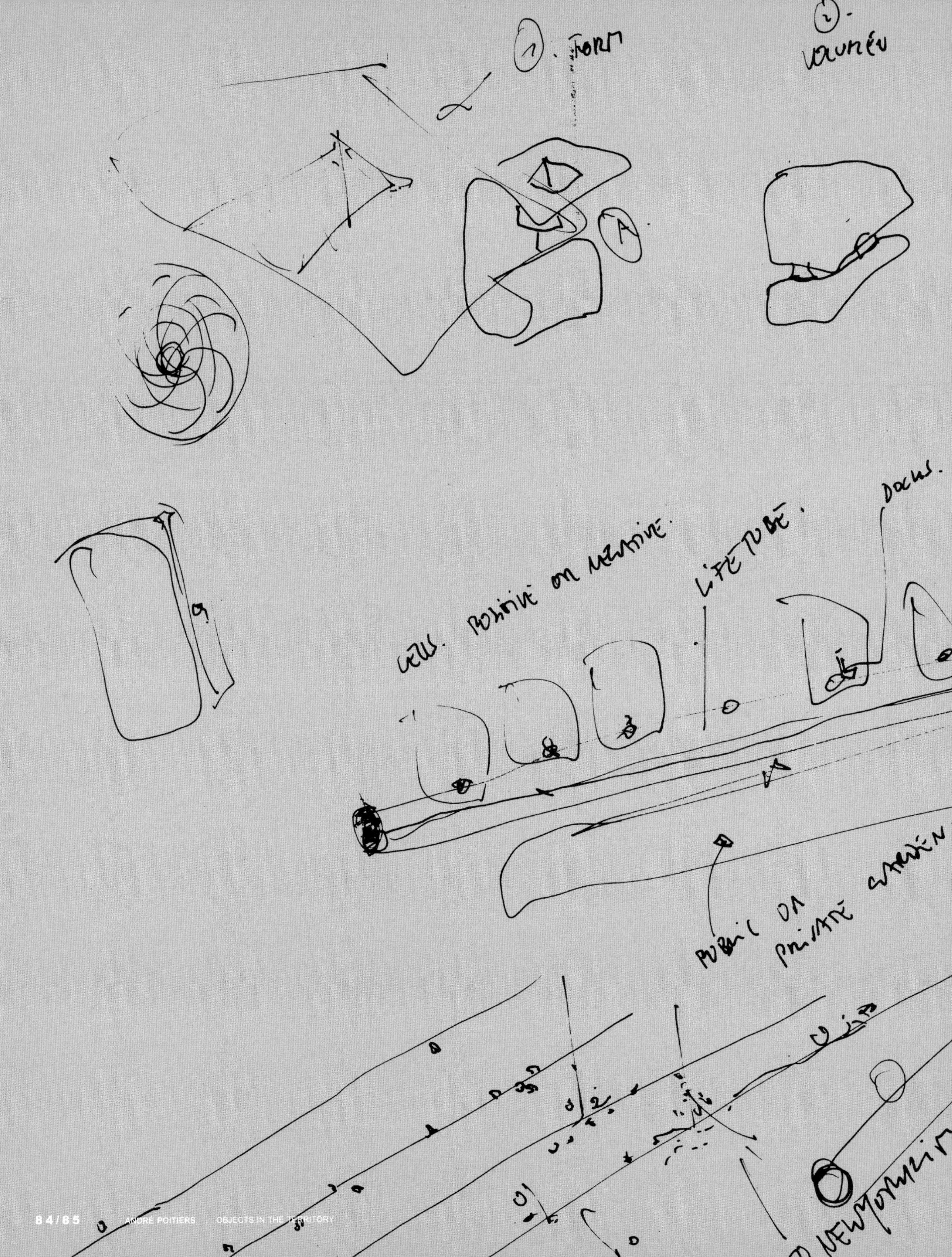
1. FORM
CELLS. POSITIVE OR NEGATIVE.
LIFE TUBE.
DOCKS.
PUBLIC OR PRIVATE GARDEN.

702-05

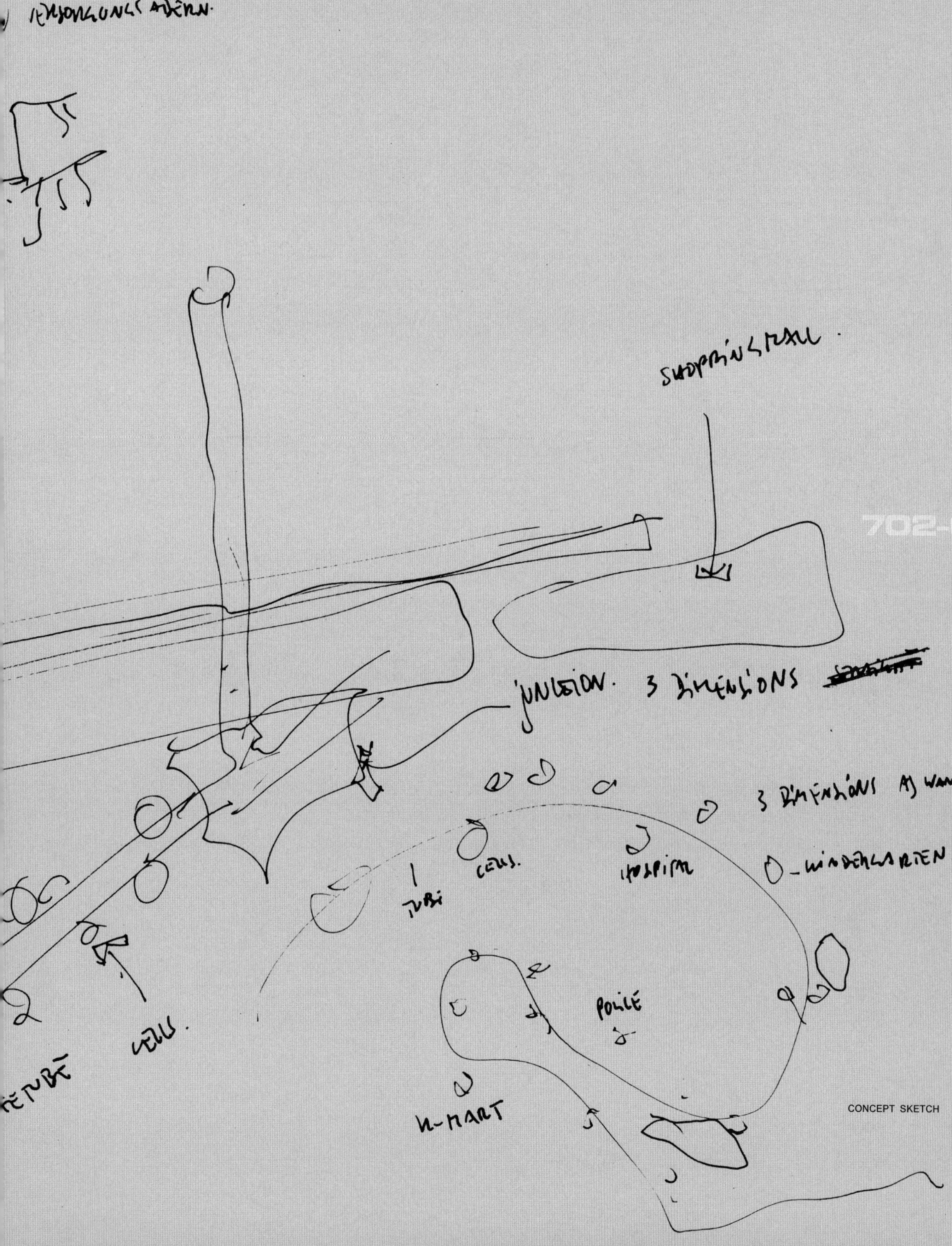

SHOPPING MALL.

JUNCTION. 3 DIMENSIONS

3 DIMENSIONS AS WANTED.

CELLS.

HOSPITAL

KINDERGARTEN.

TUBE

CELLS.

TUBE

POLICE

K-MART

CONCEPT SKETCH

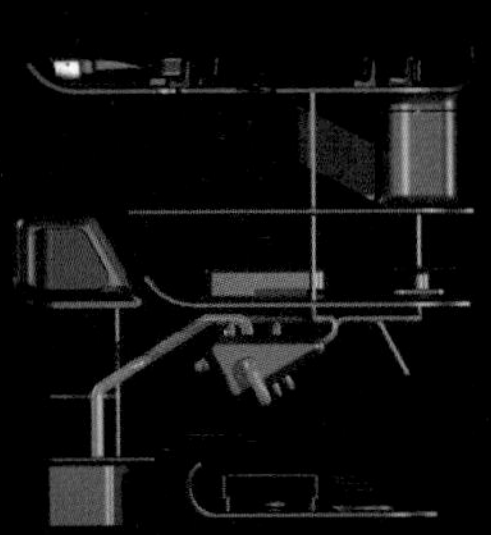

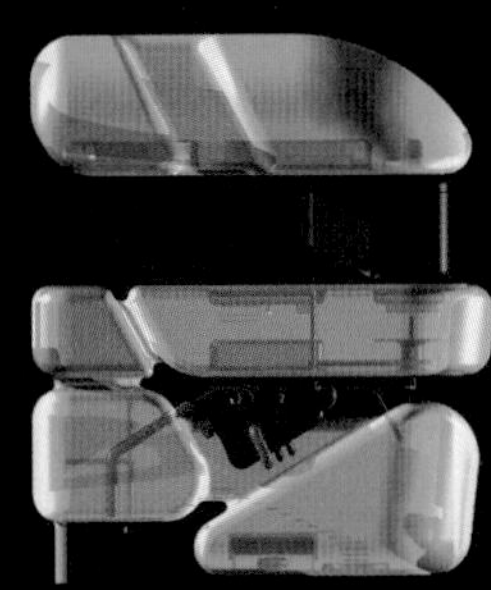

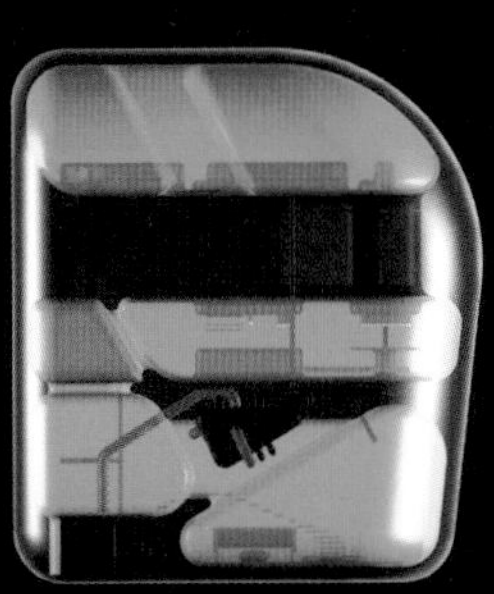

TRANSFORMATION PROCESS

702-05

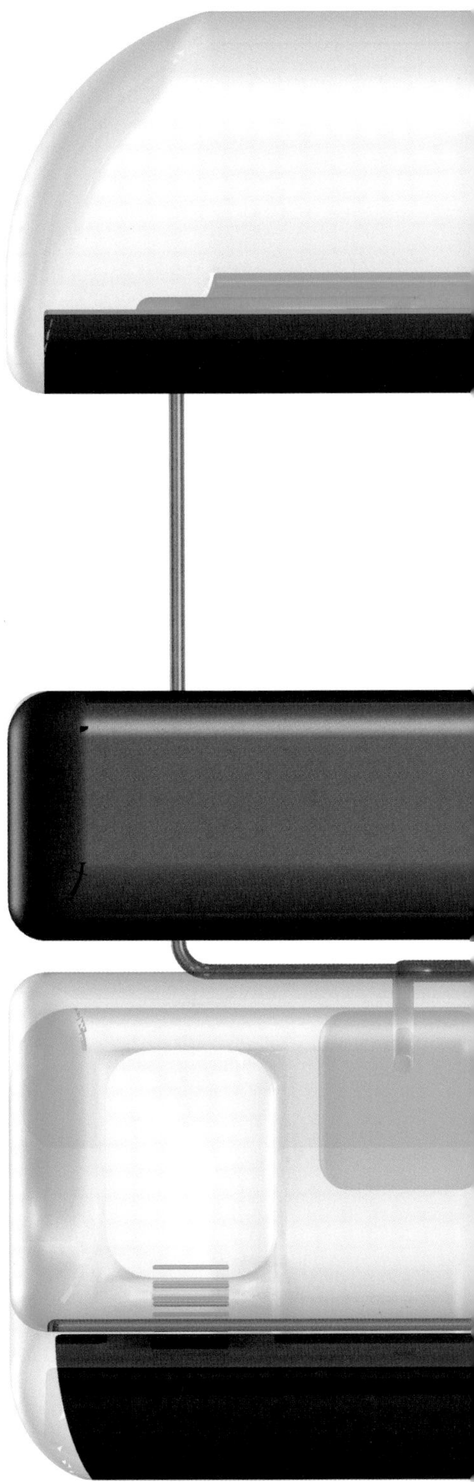

702-05

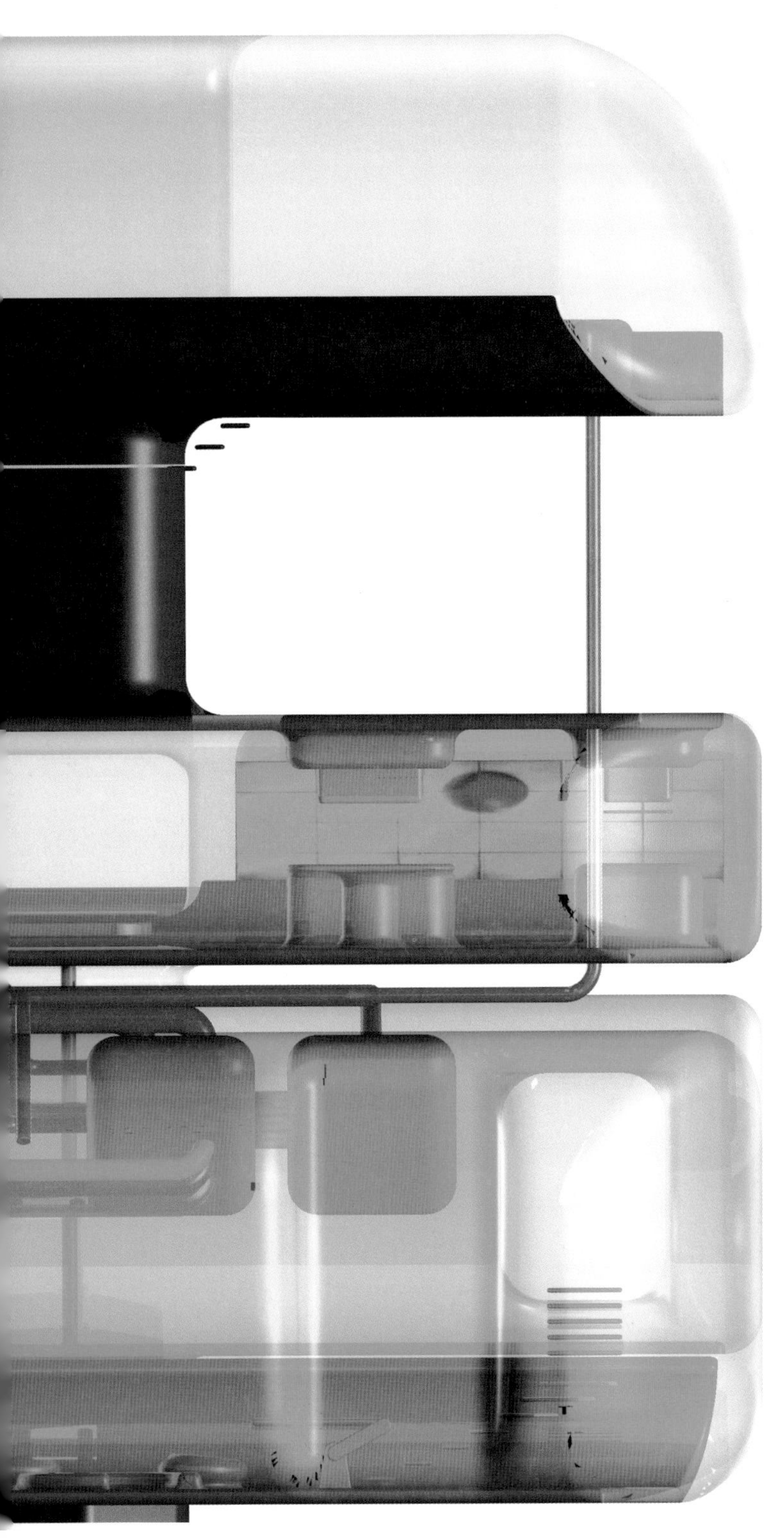

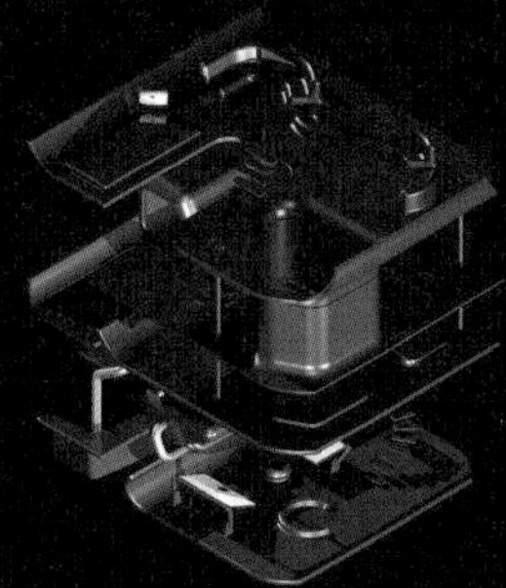

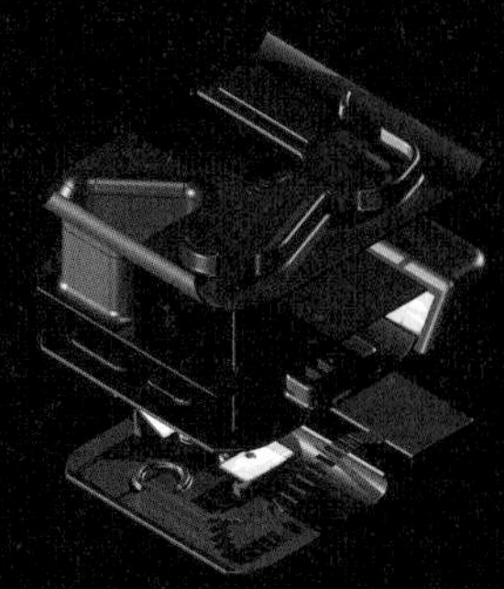

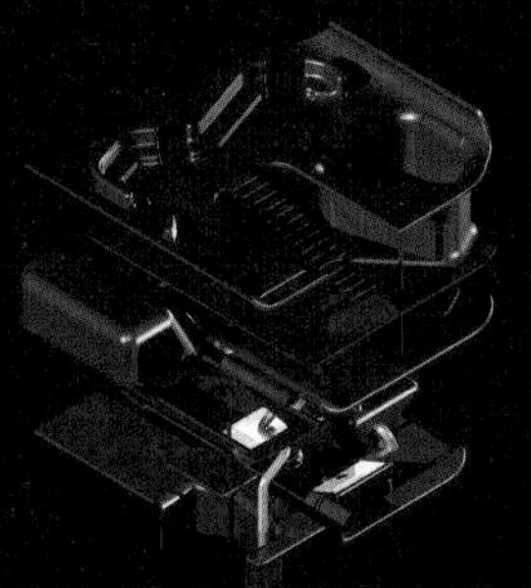

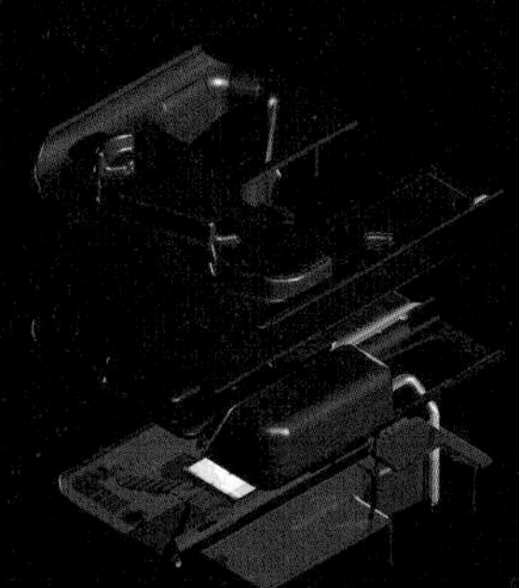

702-05

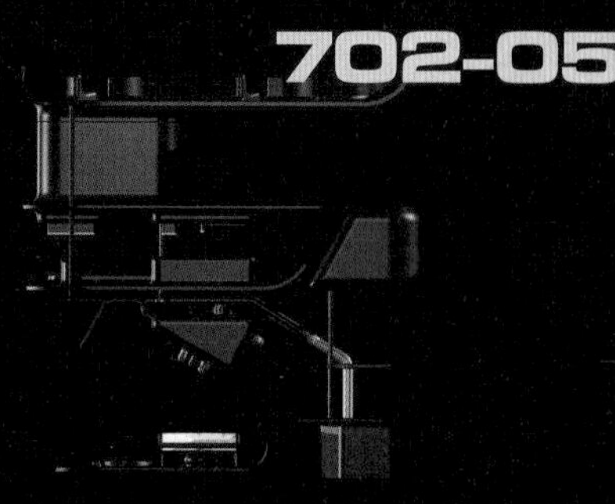

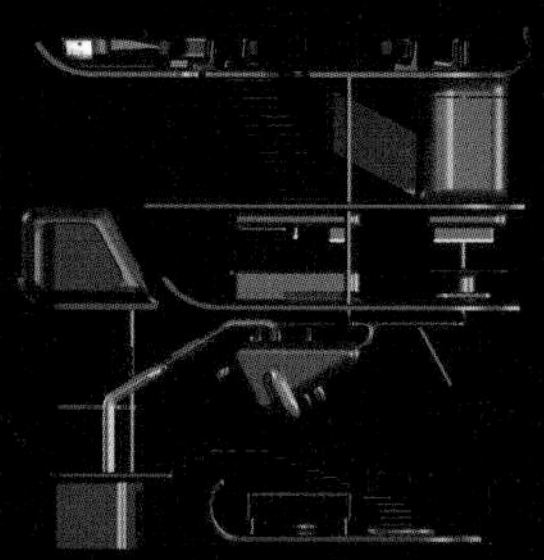

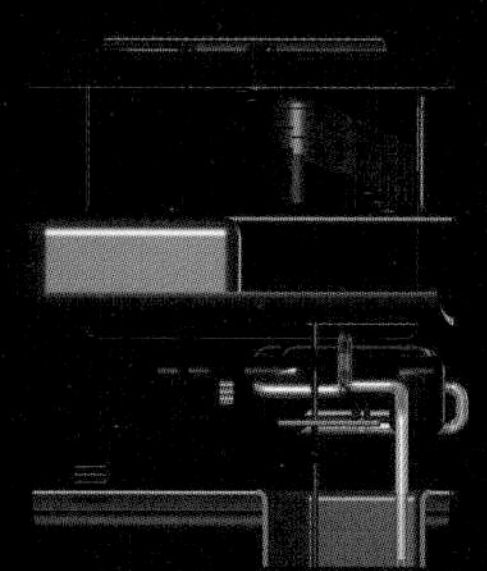

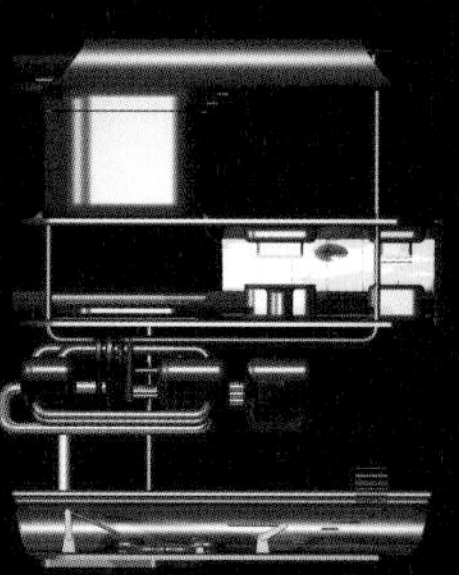

ISOMETRIC VIEWS AND ELEVATION OF THE SUBSTRUCTURE

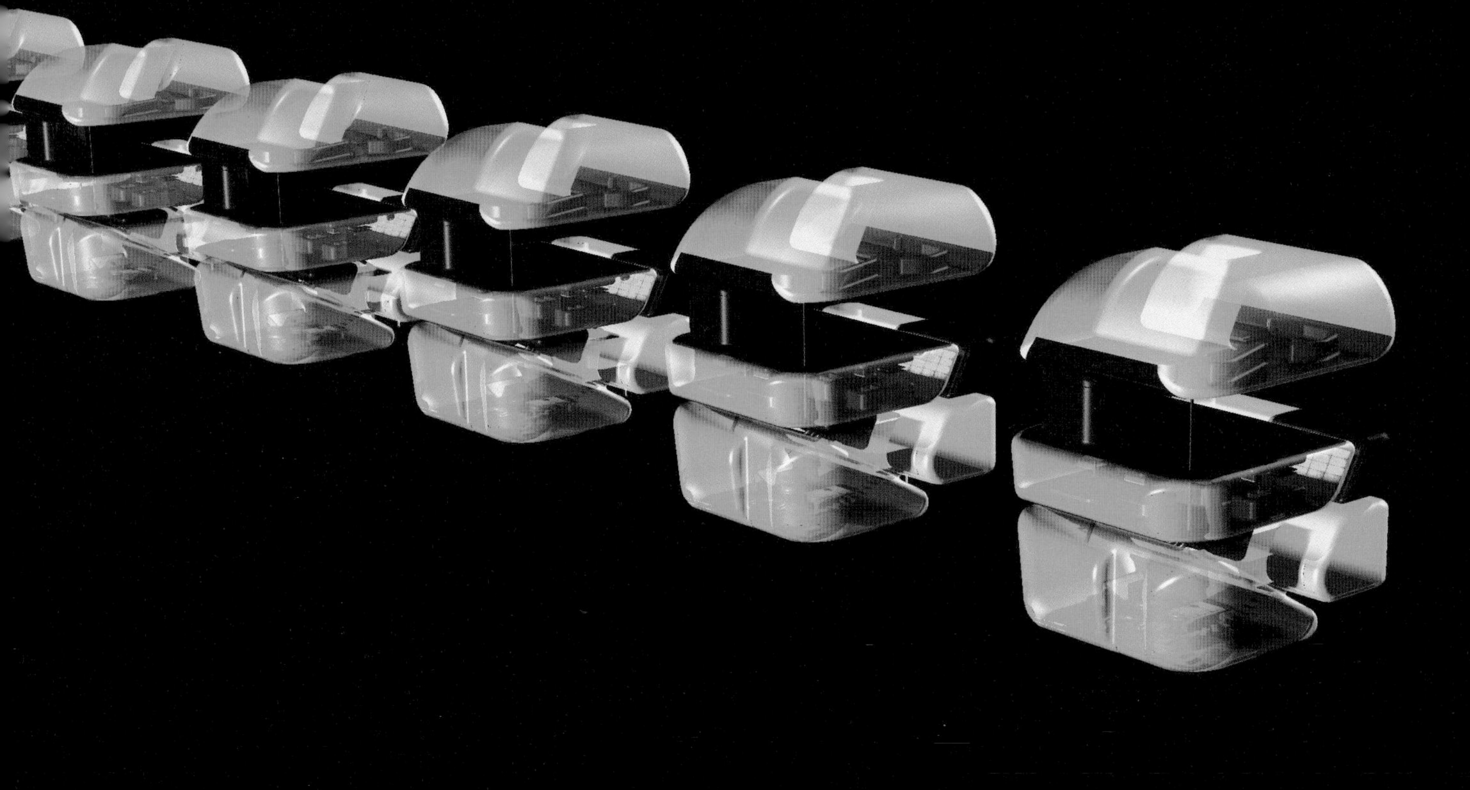

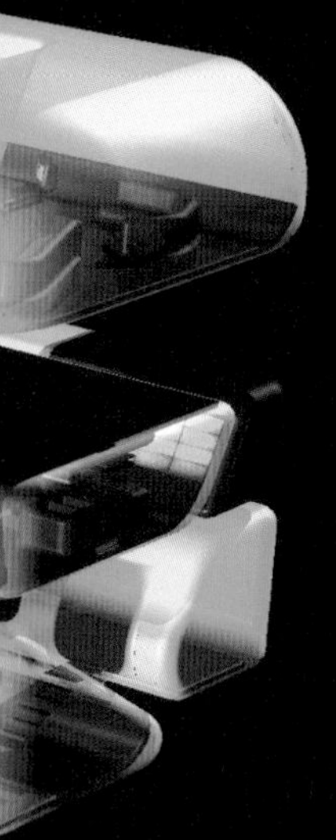

702-05

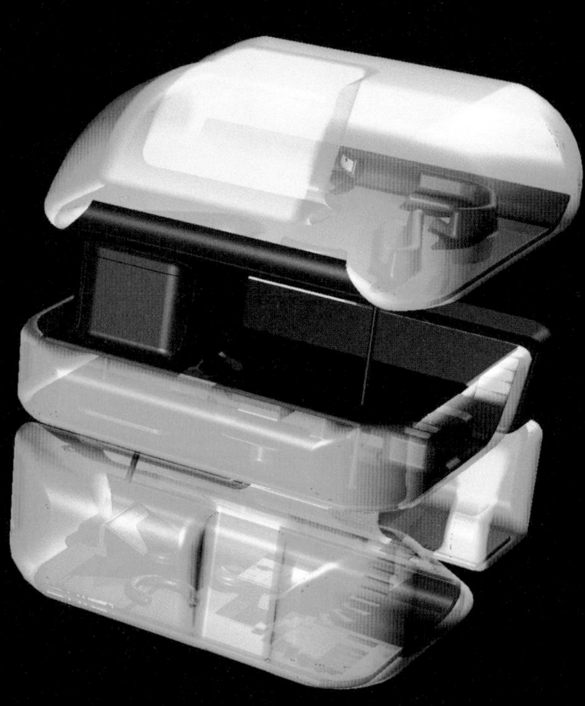

310-06

DÜSSELDORF / 2000

SPORTS & ART HOTEL

310-06

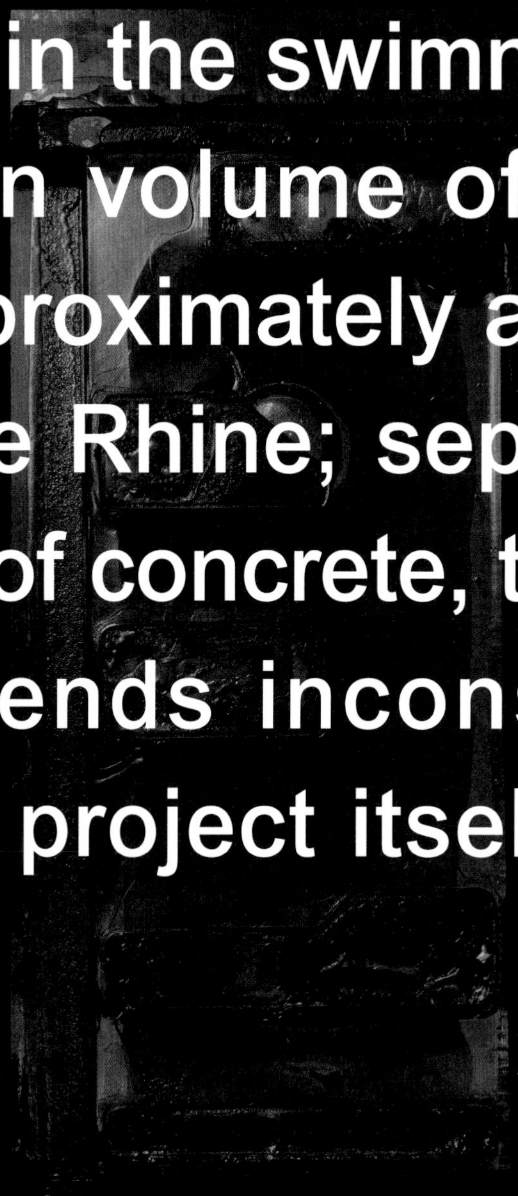

The water in the swimming pool in the sunken volume of the health club is approximately at the water-level of the Rhine; separated only by a layer of concrete, the site condition extends inconspicuously within the project itself.

HARBOURING THE BODY

For over ten years now Düsseldorf has been working on its ambitious urban development project for transforming the part of the Rhine harbour nearest the city into a "media and creative mile". Distinguished architects like Frank Gehry, Steven Holl, David Chipperfield, Claude Vasconi and others were invited to provide signature projects for a new quarter that will bring central Düsseldorf closer to the Rhine.

The Sports and Art Hotel, located on the prominent tip of the harbour pier in Speditionstrasse, completes this programmatic redefinition of the harbour with a hotel complex including a health centre and fitness studio. To exploit the location's special potential vis-à-vis the large area of the Rhine meadows, the individual functions are housed in separate volumes and staggered spatially over the plot. The high-rise hotel is twice as high as the historical development, and fills in the last gap in the double-loaded perimeter block of the pier. The remaining irregular triangle of the site thus remains intelligible as a plane forming an urban square relating to the open space of the water. The compact box for the fitness studio sits on this plate like an open-air sculpture. The health club, on the other hand, is not an independent volume, but is placed under the plate at the pointed end of the pier. A floating bridge links the complex with the bank of the harbour that has already been developed.

In architectural terms, the individual parts of the programme for the hotel differ tremendously in concept. The hotel itself is essentially a high-rise building based on a generic grid. Plastic space capsules are driven into its geometrical order, cutting large pochés out of the stacked floor structure. Arranged directly behind the façade, the public rooms in the hotel programme break the vertical seriality of the high-rise building and give its volume a three-dimensional transparency.

By contrast, the fitness centre is almost hermetically sealed off from the outside world. Several monolithic cast forms make up a technoid organic body which is presented in the neutral glass cover like an anatomical specimen. Here the rhetoric of transparency causes the internal life of the building to be concealed all the more effectively; the exhibitionism of the performing bodies can only make an impact inside.

The hotel and the fitness centre are isolated from each other above the ground as autonomous objects, but connected underground. This invisible landscape is first revealed in the health area, which is placed in the ground space under the open plateau and connected with the fitness centre. To make room for it the plateau rises from the level of the square at the tip of the pier, and the crack in the ground that this opens up is closed with a glass façade running all the way round. The water in the swimming pool behind it is approximately at the water-level of the Rhine; separated only by a layer of concrete, the site condition extends inconspicuously within the project itself.

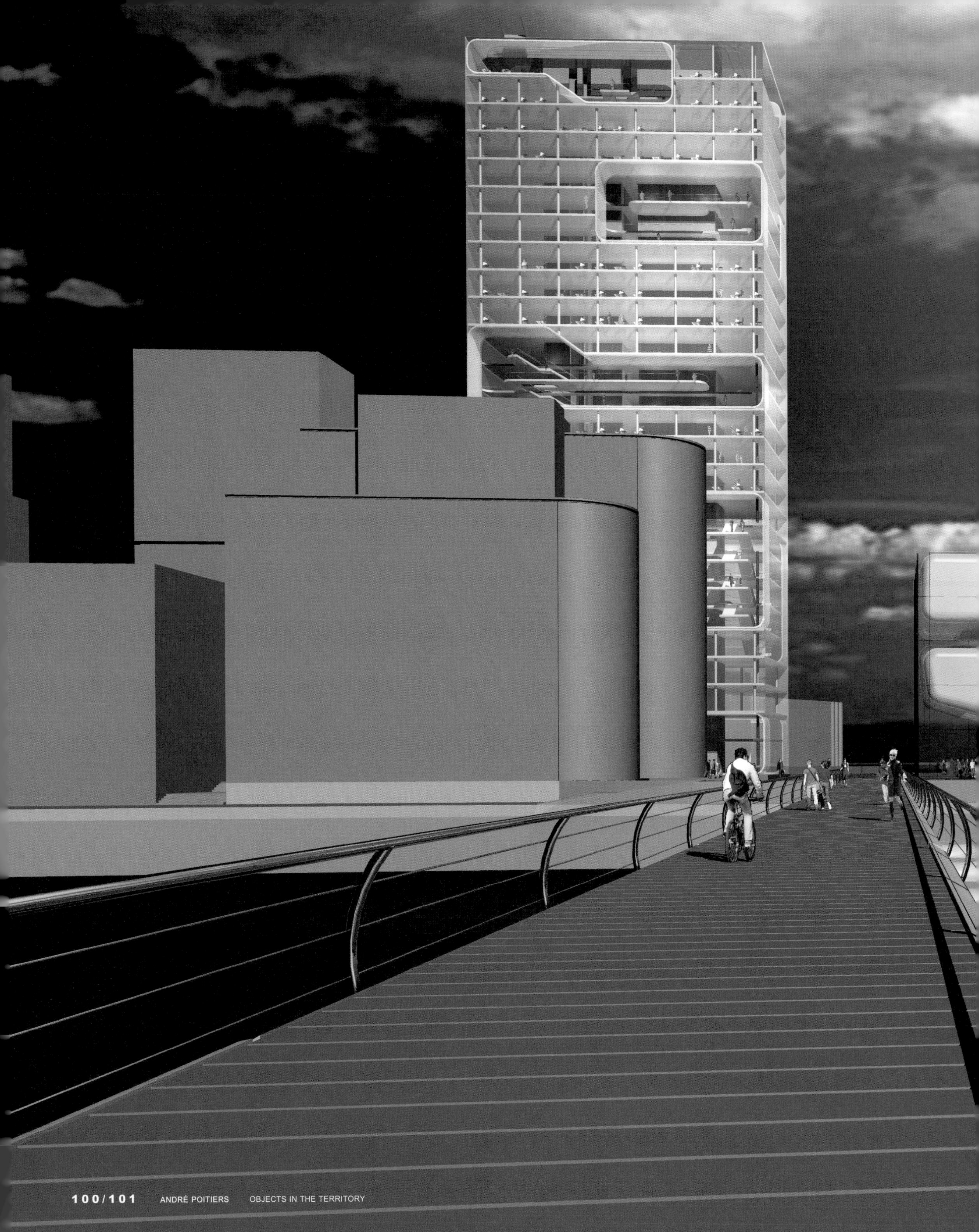

VIEW OF THE PIER TIP IN SPEDITIONSTRASSE FROM THE NEW PEDESTRIAN BRIDGE

LONGITUDINAL SECTION THROUGH THE BUILDINGCOMPLEX
AND MODEL PHOTOGRAPH

310-06

SYNTHETIC RESIN MOULDS FOR THE MODEL OF THE HIGH-RISE BUILDING

310-06

STRUCTURE OF THE HIGH-RISE BUILDING WITH AND WITHOUT FLOORS AND CORE

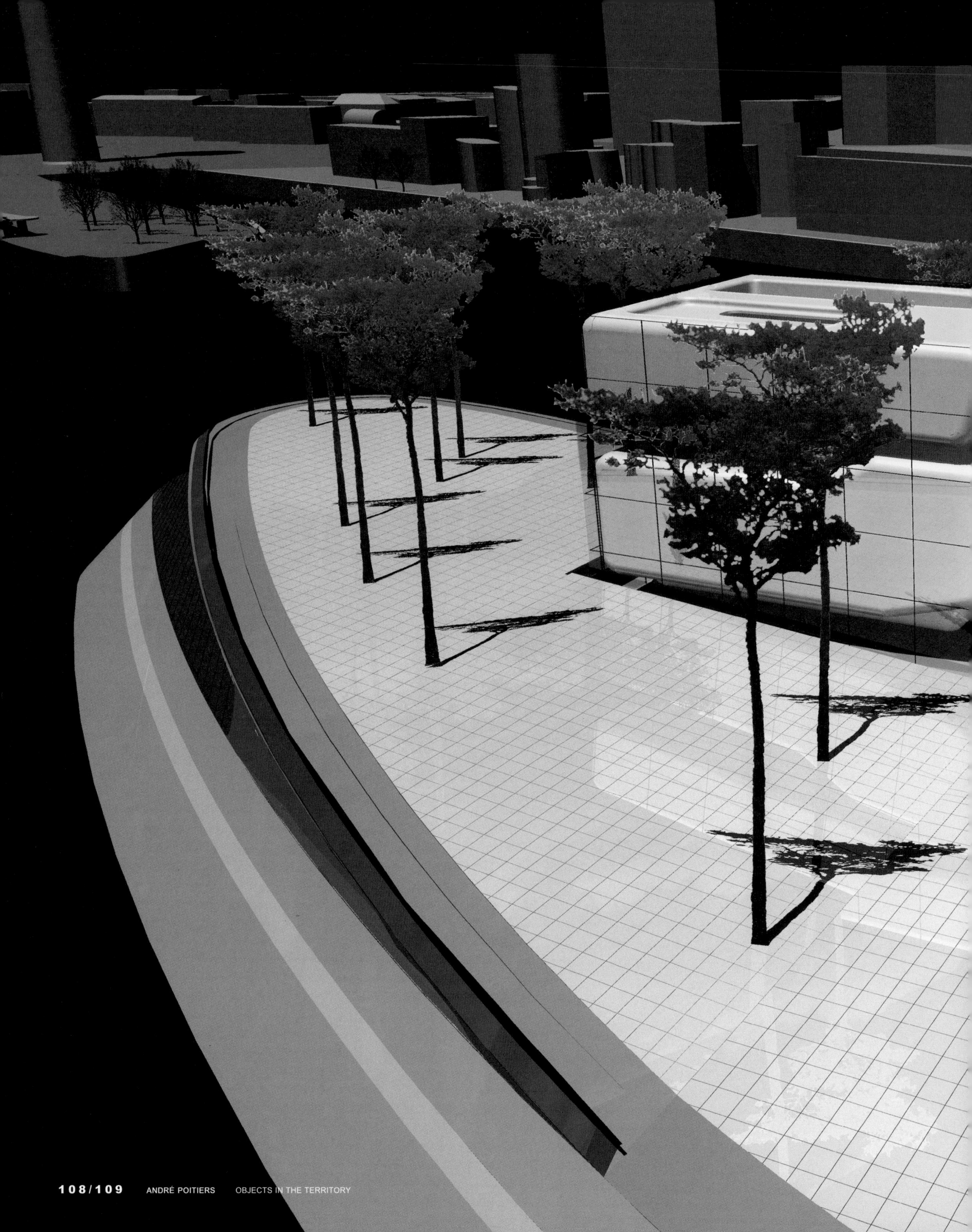

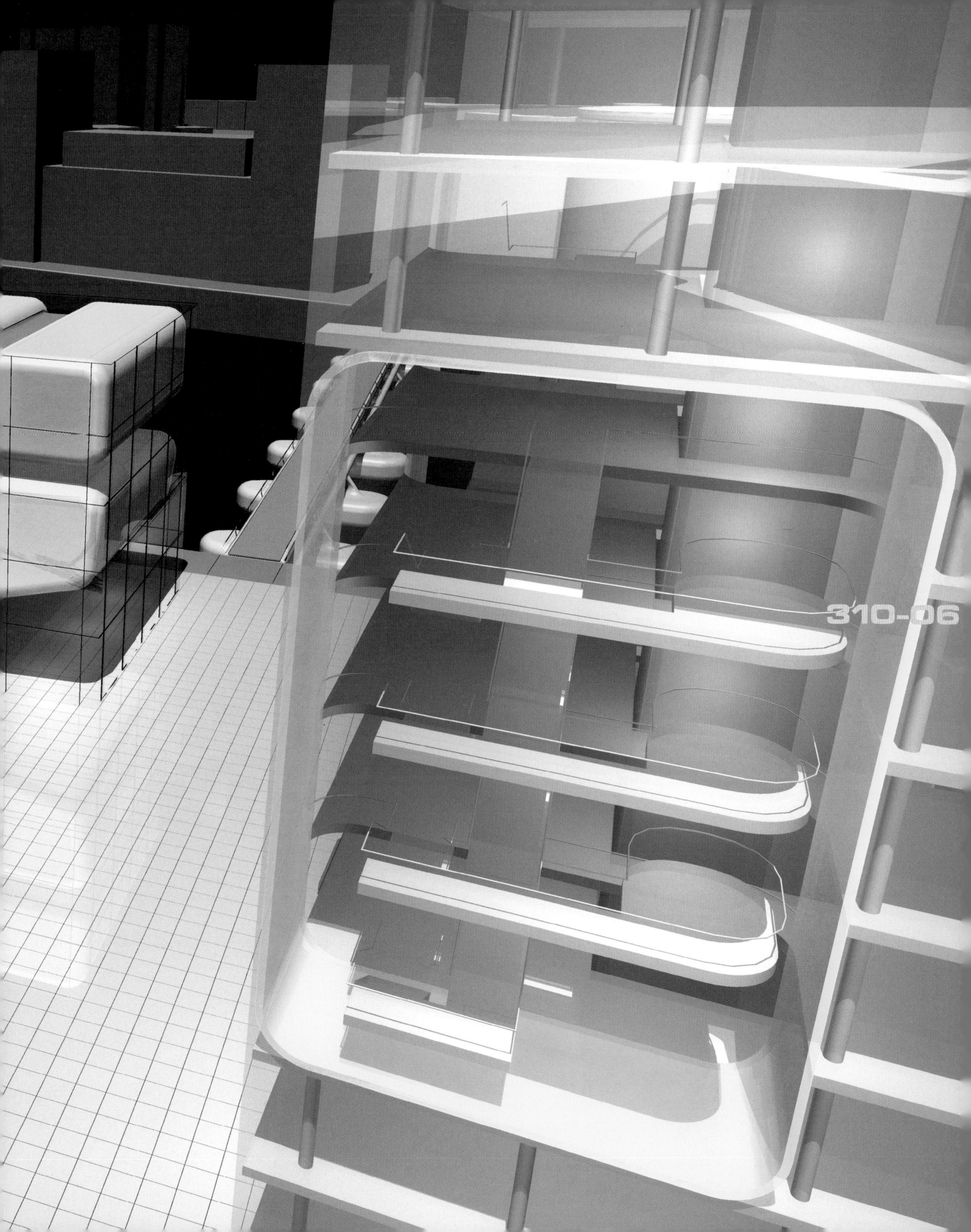
310-06

310-06

308-07

SHOPPING MALL & OFFICE BUILDING / YOKOHAMA / 2000

MM 18-21

308-07

Rather than a building in a city, this is more like a city in a building, combining and transforming public spaces into a meta-interior. An urban biotope under its own sky which surrounds the inner life of the building like the cocoon of an insect's egg.

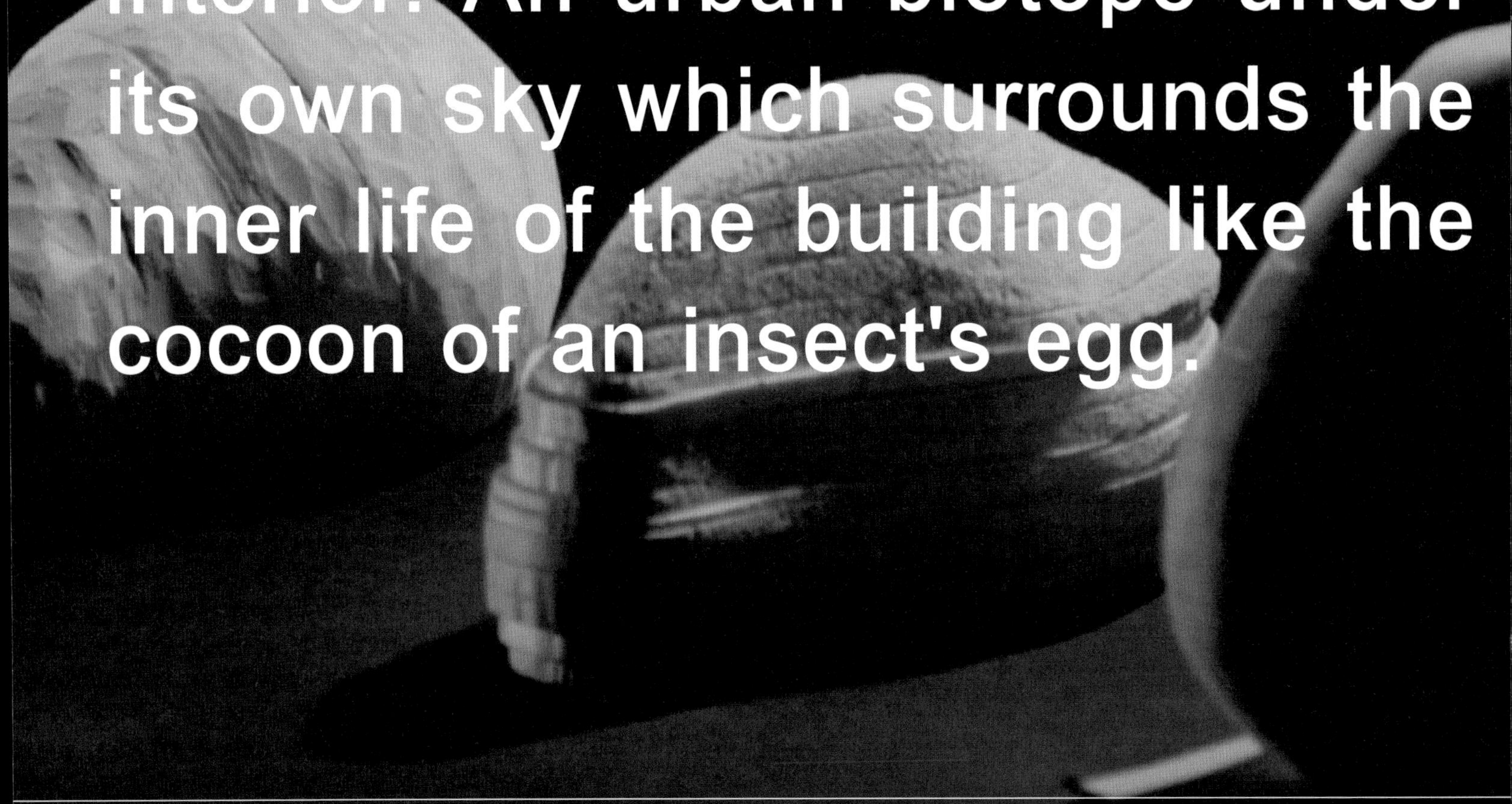

FROZEN EGG CELL

This project emerged after the Plasma House, and was developed on the same design principle, though not worked out in detail. Here too the building was first devised as pure form without a defined function. The volume produced is first of all a body without scale; its actual physical size is not defined until it is related to the scale of the site and the programme, and thus scaled up accordingly. This produces a monstrously large structure that is zoned in terms of functions in the next step, leading to a transformation of the volume. Shopping is placed at the bottom, with dwellings and offices above; between them the multiplex cinema carves an open space out of the mass of the building. Given the enormous dimensions, the project tends to transcend the status of a building. Instead of a building in a city, this is more like a city in a building. This hybridization of building and urban space is reminiscent of Buckminster Fuller's transparent dome over New York: the cover brings urban spaces together and transforms them into a meta-interior, an urban biotope under its own sky. But while Fuller's dome floats over the city like a halved soap bubble, in Poitiers' case it surrounds the building like the cocoon of an insect's egg, thus accentuating the interface between indoor and outdoor urban space. At the moment the project is still at an intermediate stage. The study was not followed by a commission, and so the design process stopped at a given point. And yet that did not mean the end of the project. Its present condition is like that of an embryo frozen after artificial insemination, so that it can be thawed out and finished off at a later stage. But then the same applies to the project as to the fertilized egg cell: the implantation point for further development has yet to be fixed. Thus the context is variable, but the form of the project binding.

308-07

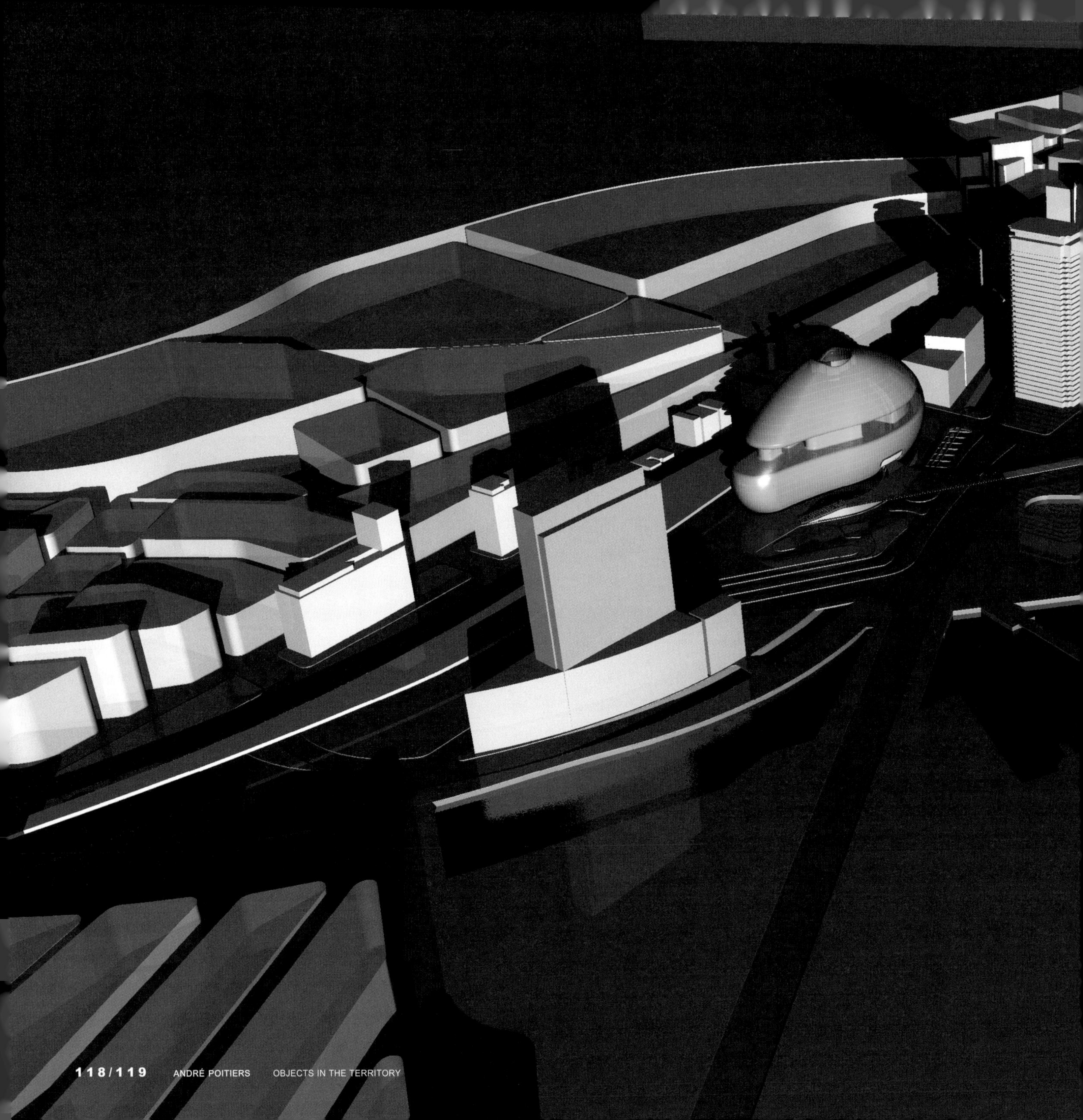

308-07

URBAN CONTEXT IN YOKOHAMA WITH BUILDING

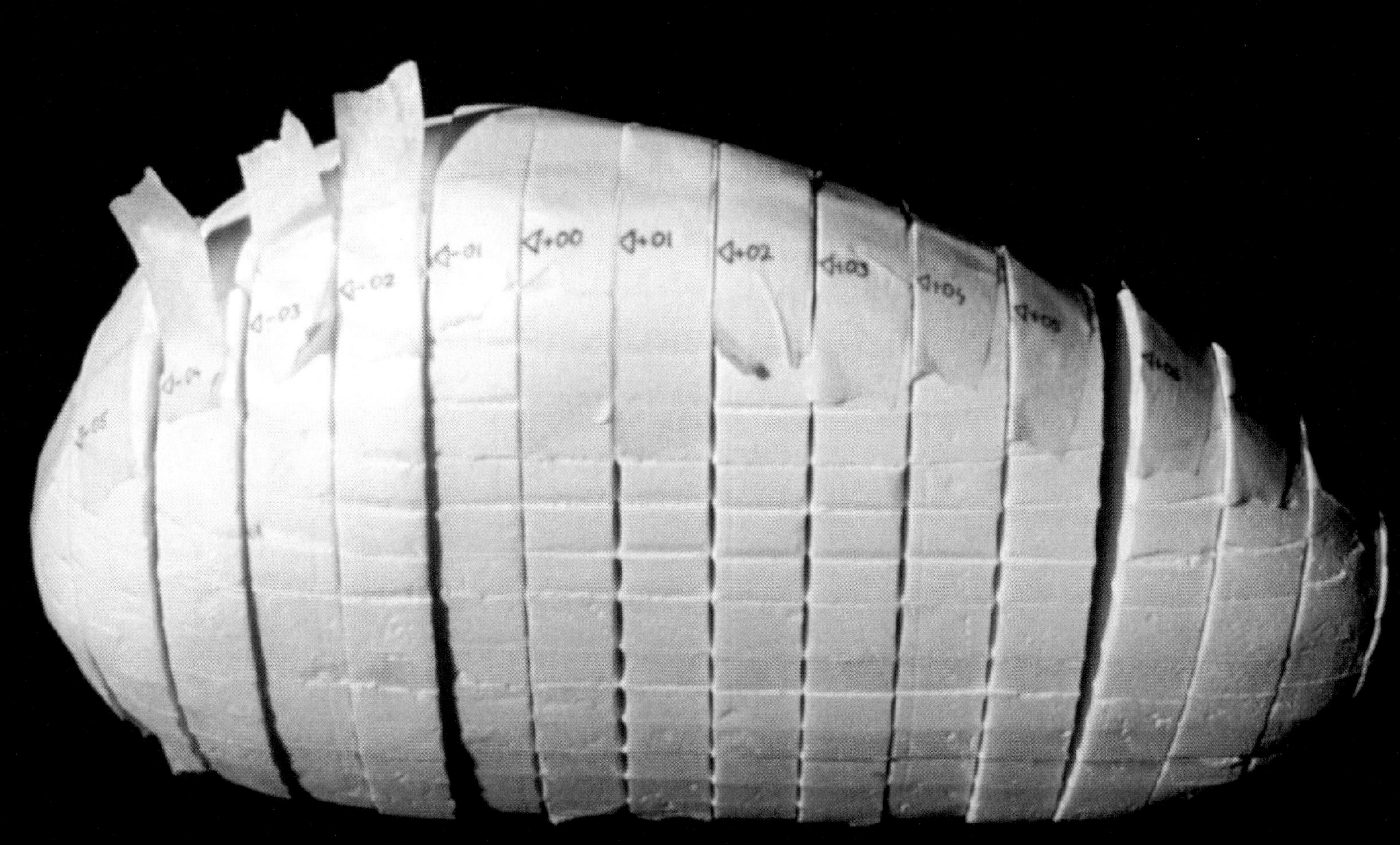
◁-03
◁-02
◁-01
◁+00
◁+01
◁+02
◁+03

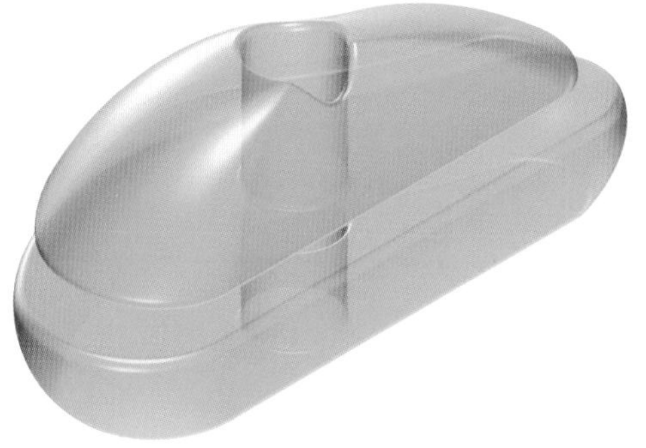

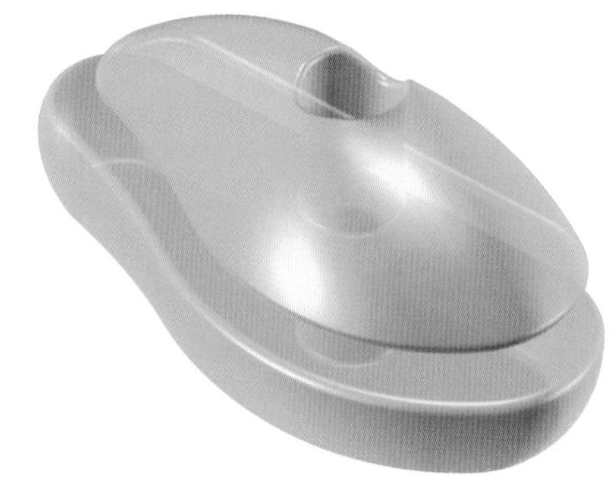

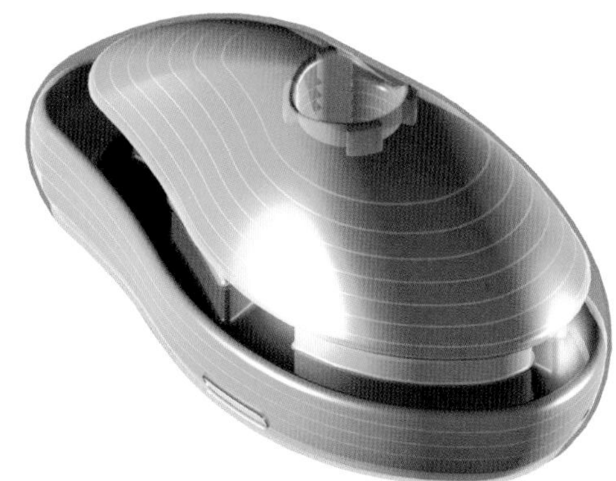

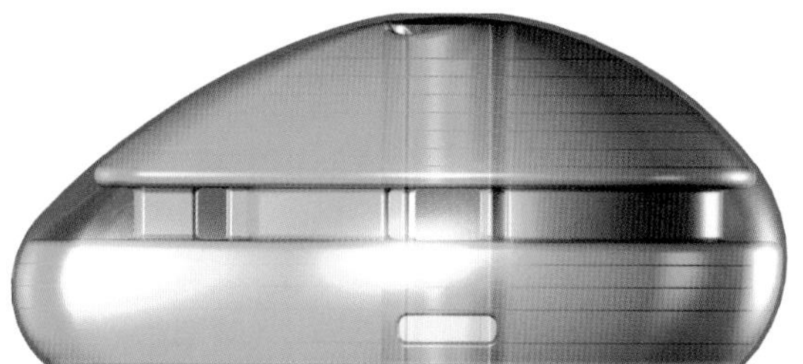

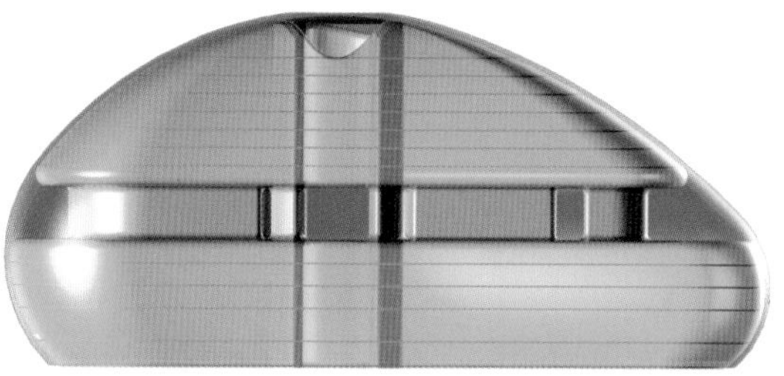

MODEL OF A BUILDING STUDY AND RENDERINGS OF THE BUILDING

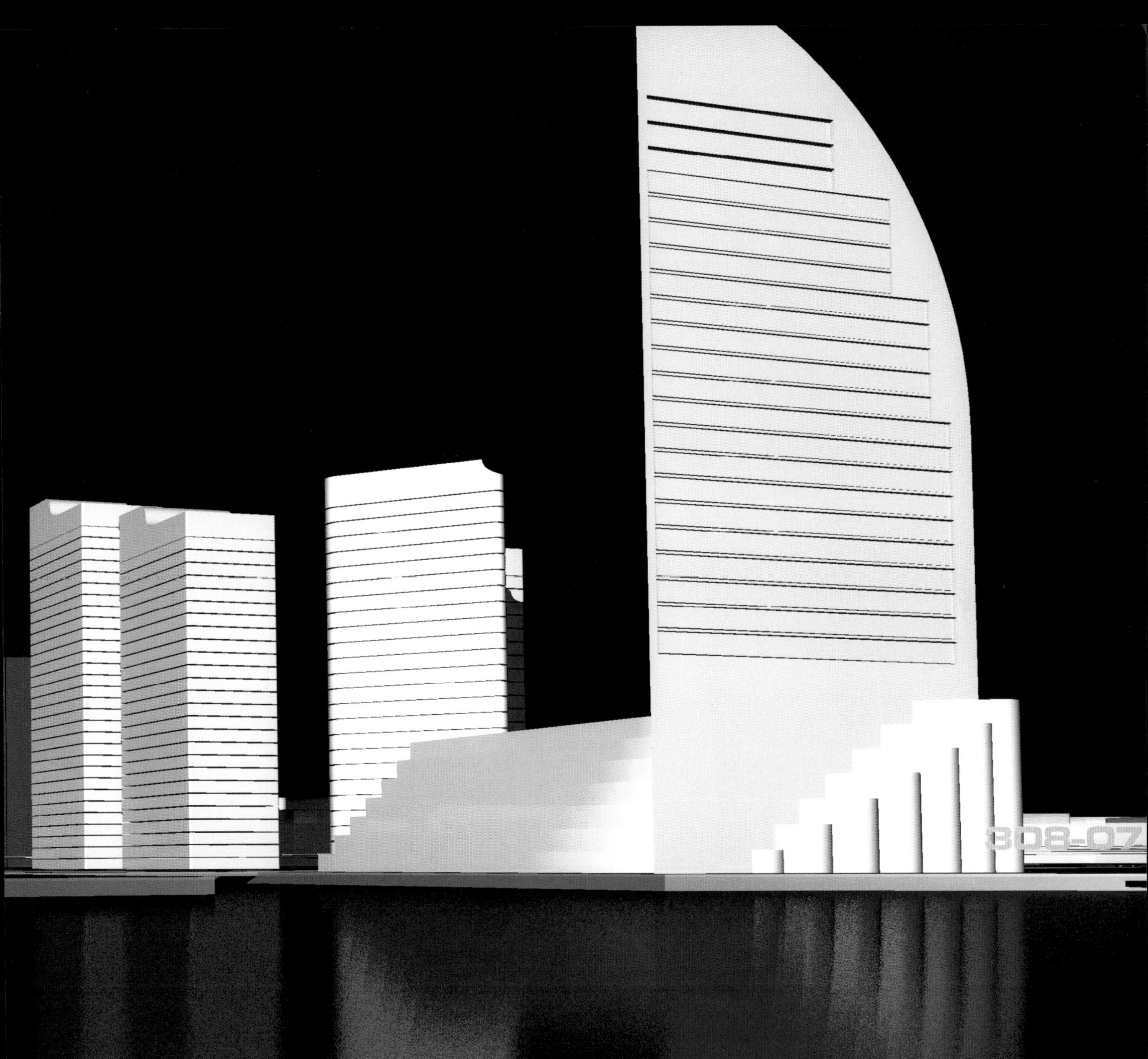
308-07

322-08

RESTAURANT / HAMBURG / 2000

CAFÉ KAJEN

CAFÉ KAJEN

322-08

By turning away from the city and opening up to the harbour the building extrapolates Hamburg's urban heterogeneity, amplifying the tension between the discip-lined perimeter block building of the historic bourgeois city and the apparently wild growth of the harbour landscape with shipyards and the container terminal.

WRAPPED VIEW

If there were no building on the plot between the harbour road and the quay wall you would scarcely be aware that it exists. We only become aware of this leftover site because of the curved shell that bends upwards towards a wall as though it had been pulled out of the ground and then finally brought back on to the horizontal to float above the plot like a magic carpet. The Café Kajen is more than a roof but less than a building, and combines the qualities of a contained space with those of an open body. In fact the design derives from the closed volume of a SIGG bottle. The precision of its all-enclosing aluminium envelope became the model for the architectural effect that the building was intended to make. The closed tube is placed at the point where the town meets the port, and starts to change when exposed to their opposing forces: while the volume opens up on the side that faces the harbour, the rest of the shell shields the newly formed space from the city. The condition of the site changes the non-directional ideal geometry of the SIGG bottle into a specific building with a front and a back. It sits on the quayside wall like the stranded hull of a boat, an aquatic structure that has ended up on land.

This transformation of a design prototype (bottle) into a structural type (ship's hull), triggered by the act of location, can also be seen in the construction method, which is very reminiscent of ship-building. The building's load-bearing structure consists of bent steel girders, fitted with aluminium L-sections to which a skin of welded aluminium sheets is fixed lengthways. Polished, smoothed, painted and lacquered, in its final state this skin gives the building the immaterial elegance of a modern hightech yacht. This affinity with material effects drawn from shipbuilding is continued inside the shell, which is covered all over with timber panels. And so the café, although it is transparently glazed on three sides, can develop a powerful interior effect that is also supported by the organization of the ground plan. Even after you have come into the building you are still outside to a certain extent. A wall running parallel with the glass façade makes it impossible to look into the café behind it from the entrance. From there the café is accessed via a ramp leading up between the inner wall and the outer façade. As you arrive on the raised level you seem to be coming into the café for the second time. It is only here that the effect made by the protruding shell roof is fully developed. And it is only from up here that the meaning of the inner wall is revealed: it modulates the transparency of the façade so that you do not feel too exposed to the outside world while in the café, but at the same time you are profoundly in touch with it.

And yet the building is not only addressing the immediately visible context. By turning away from the city and opening up to the harbour the building is also extrapolating the heterogeneity of Hamburg's urban quality: the tension between the disciplined perimeter block building of the historic bourgeois city on the one hand and the apparently wild growth of the harbour landscape with shipyards and the container terminal on the other. Café Kajen sits on the quay like a container itself, suggesting that it is more in sympathy with the world of the harbour than the built urban space.

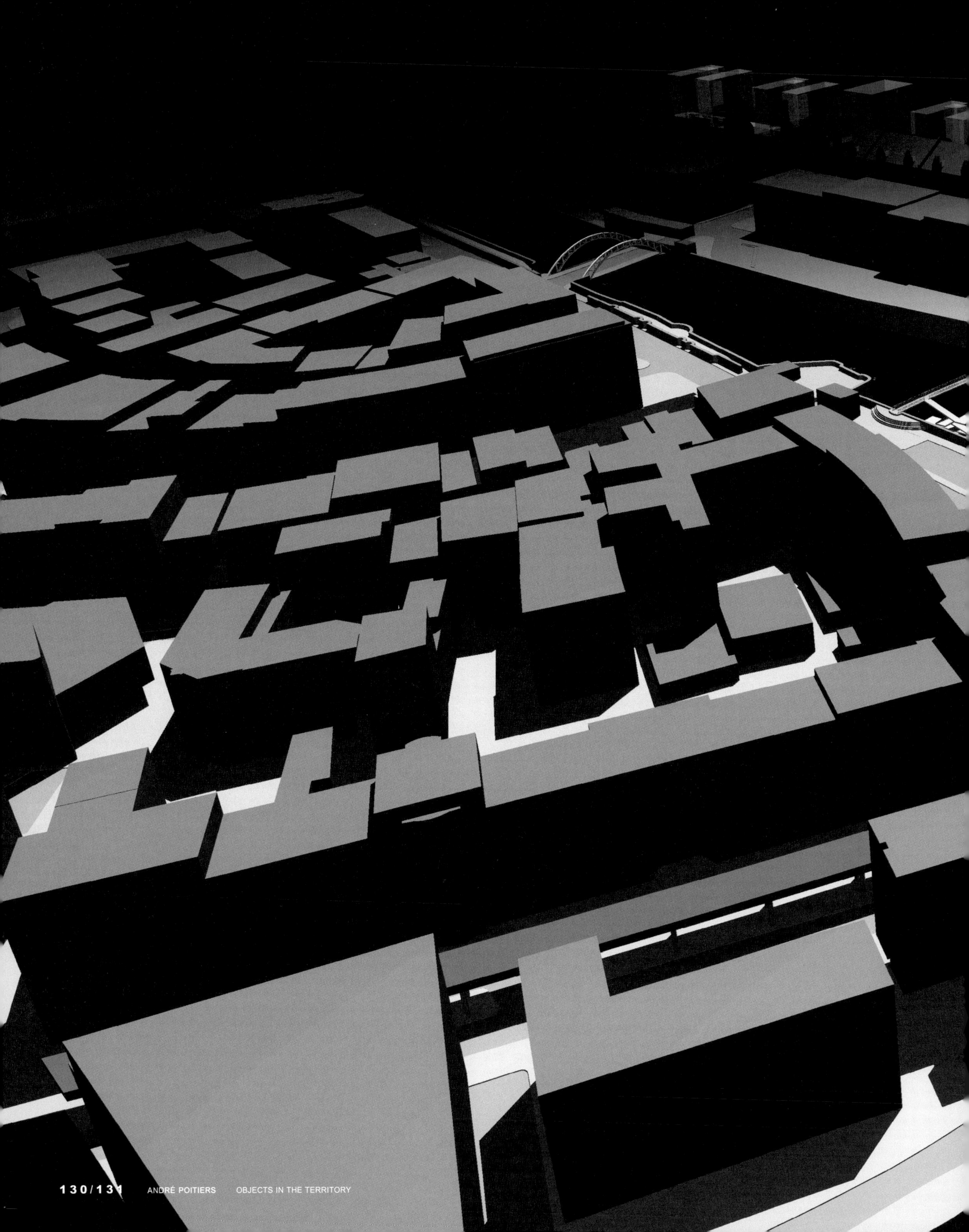

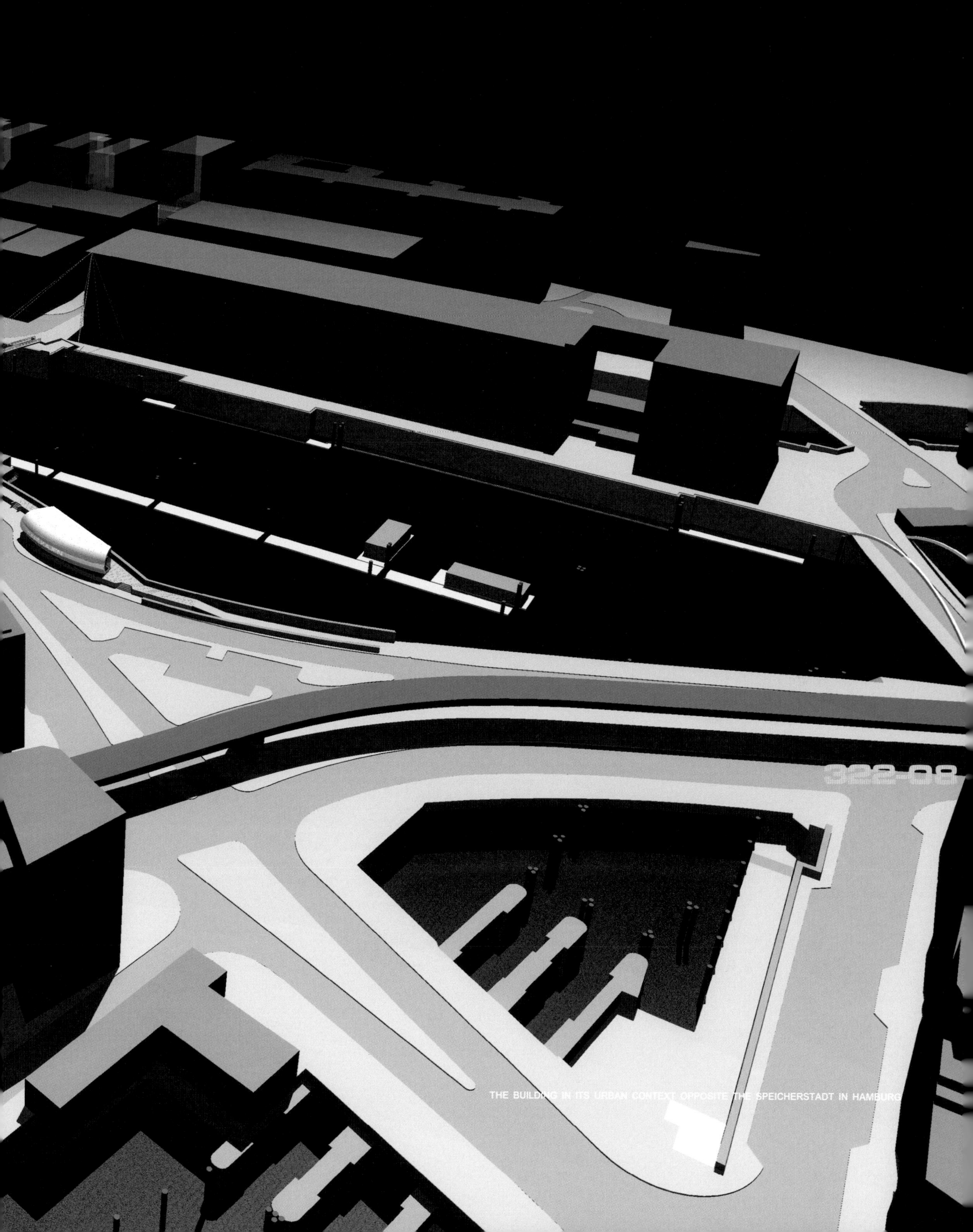

THE BUILDING IN ITS URBAN CONTEXT OPPOSITE THE SPEICHERSTADT IN HAMBURG

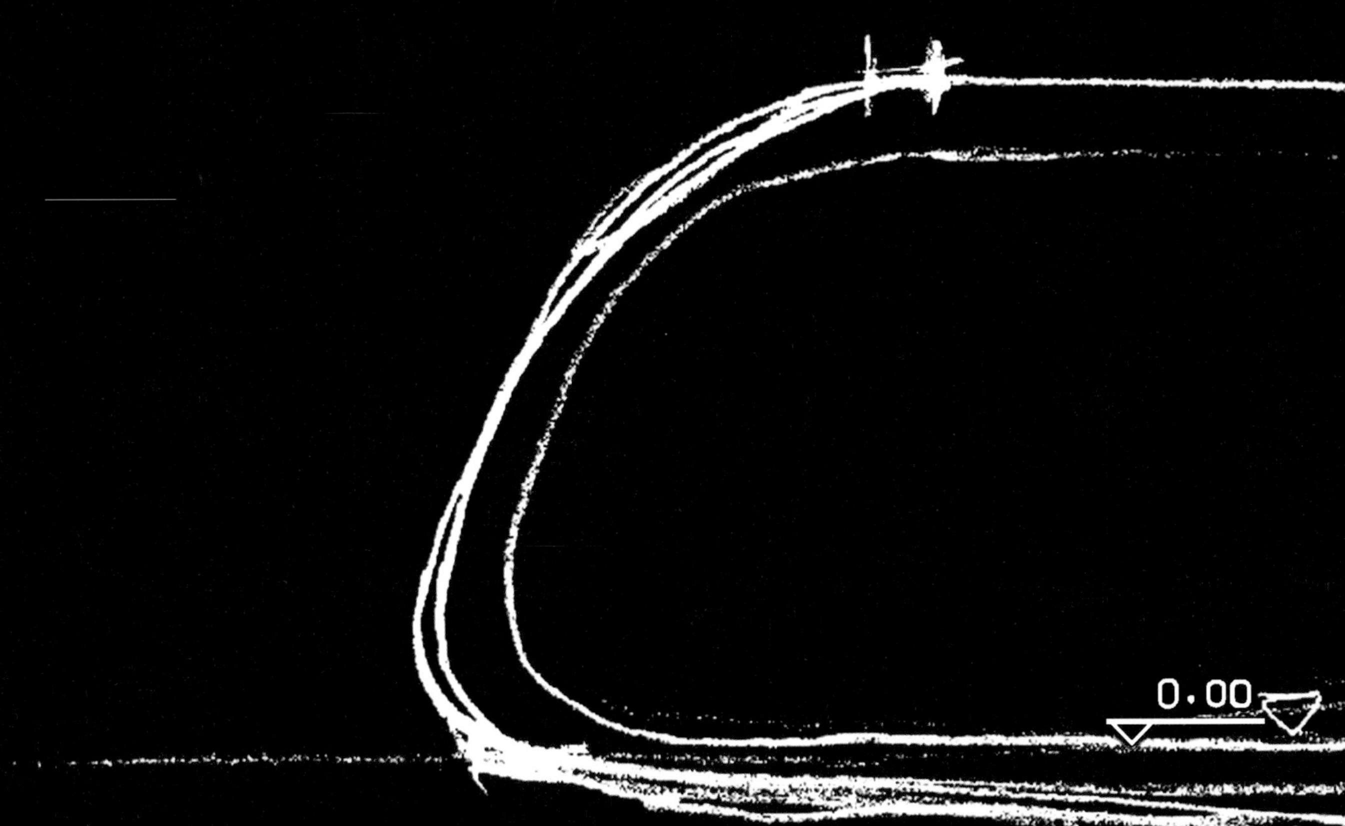
0.00

+5.00

322-08

DESIGN SKETCH

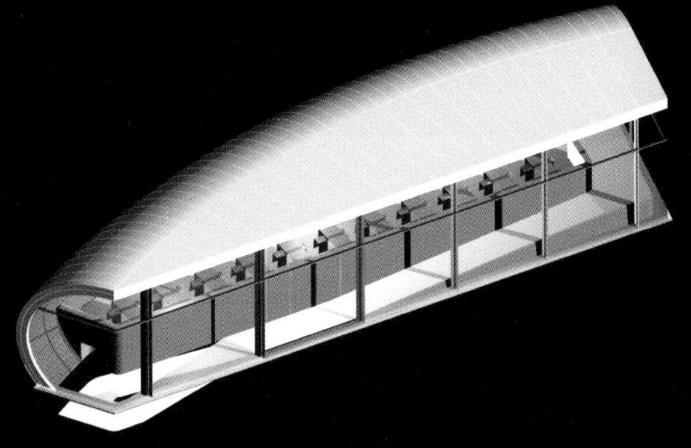

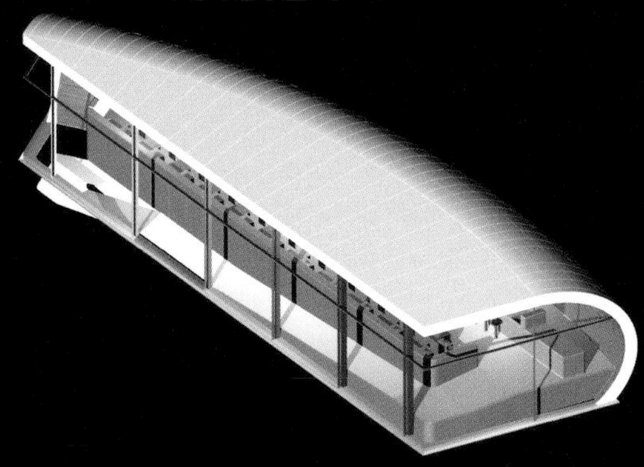

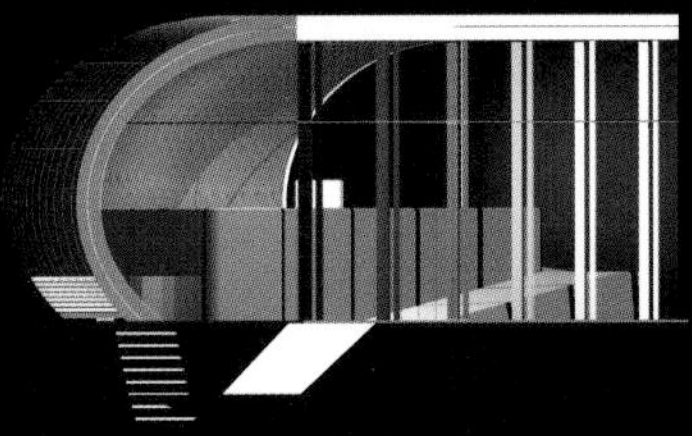

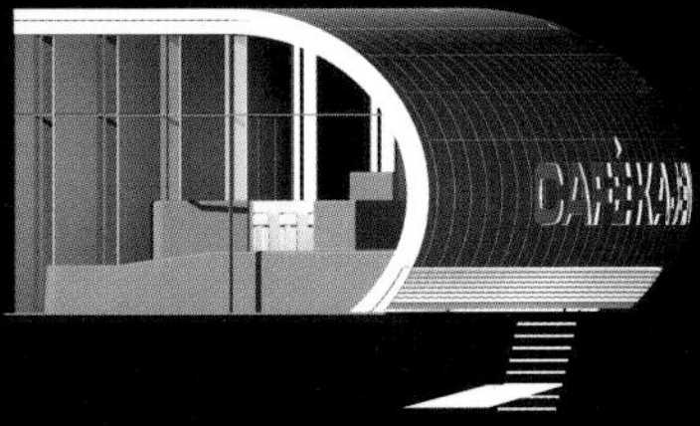

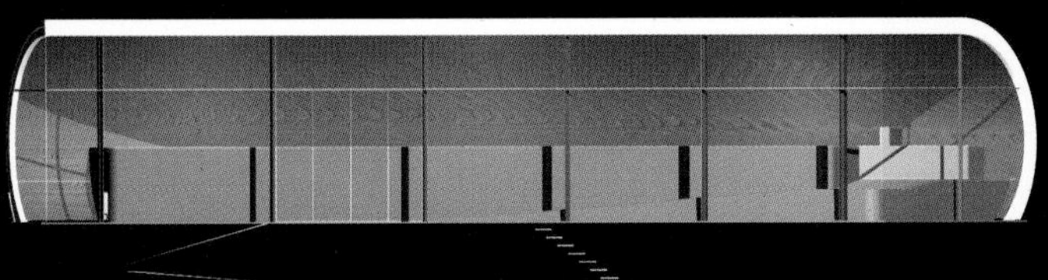

ISOMETRIC VIEWS AND ELEVATIONS OF THE BUILDING

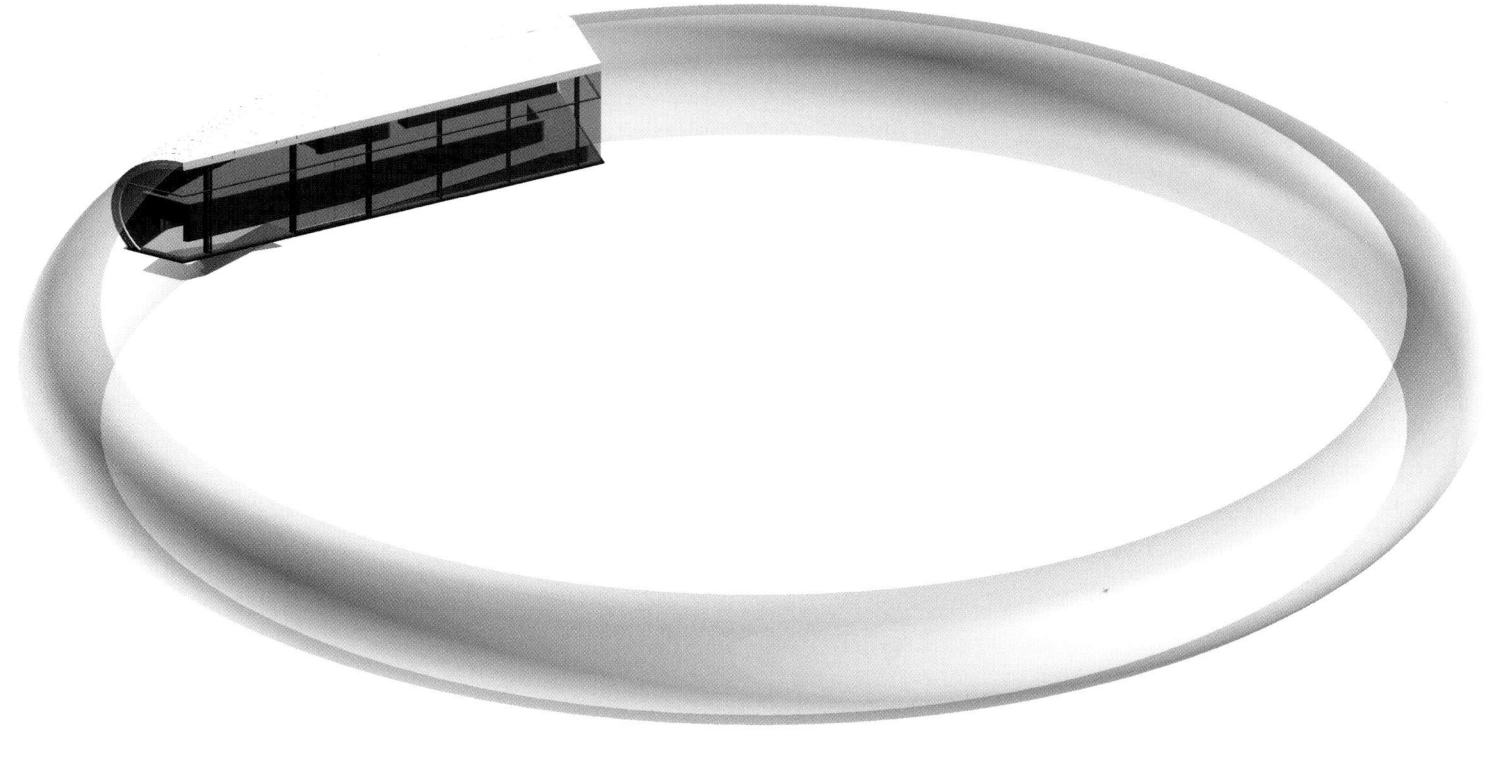

322-08

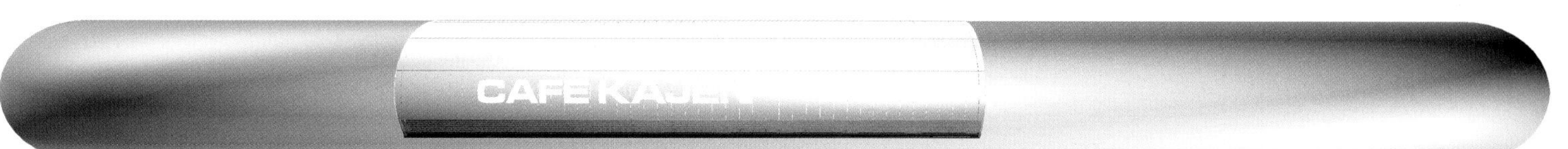

THE GEOMETRICAL BASIS OF THE BUILDING SHOWN AS A SEGMENT OF A CIRCLE

MODEL PHOTOGRAPH AND GROUND PLAN

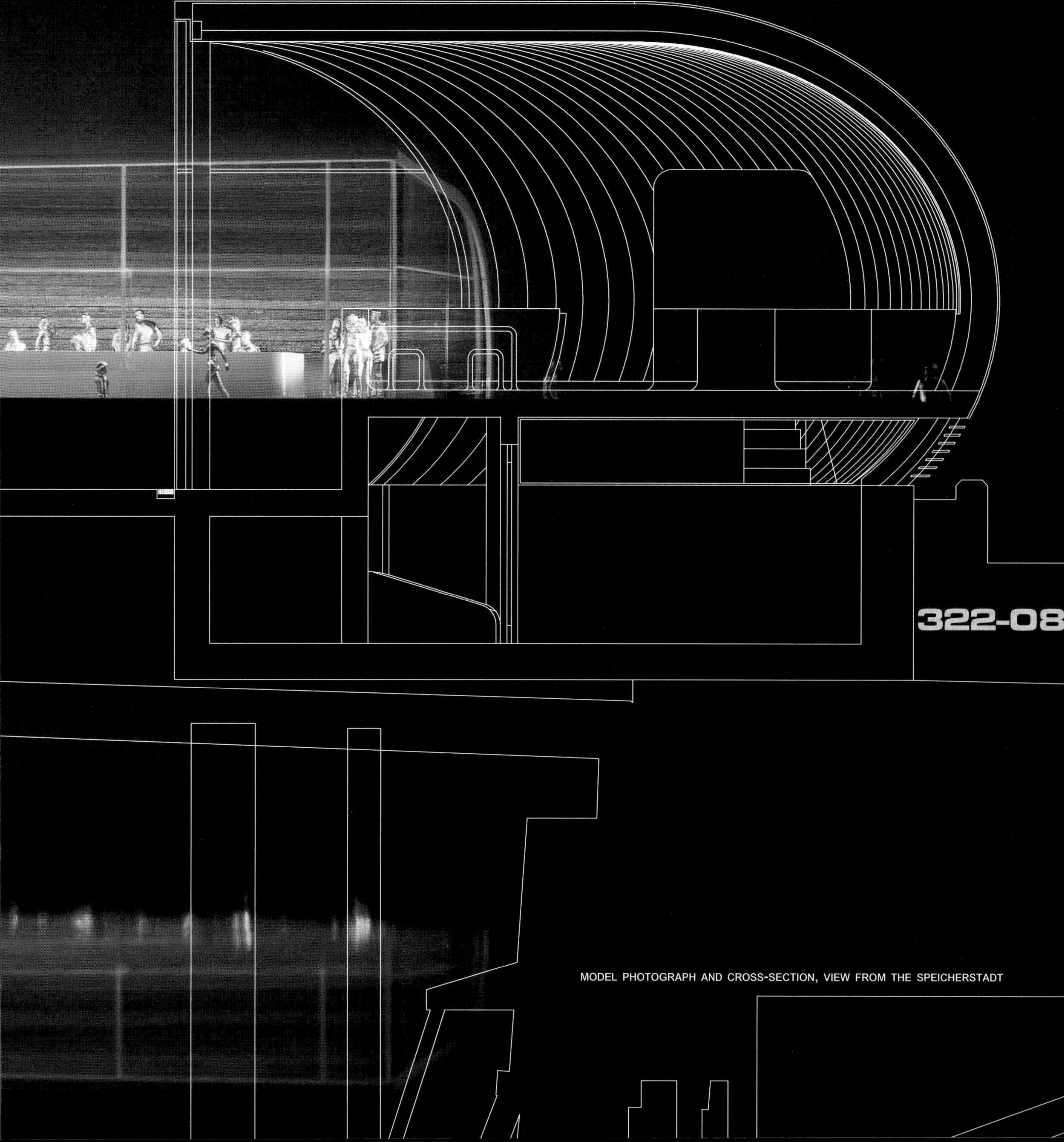

MODEL PHOTOGRAPH AND CROSS-SECTION, VIEW FROM THE SPEICHERSTADT

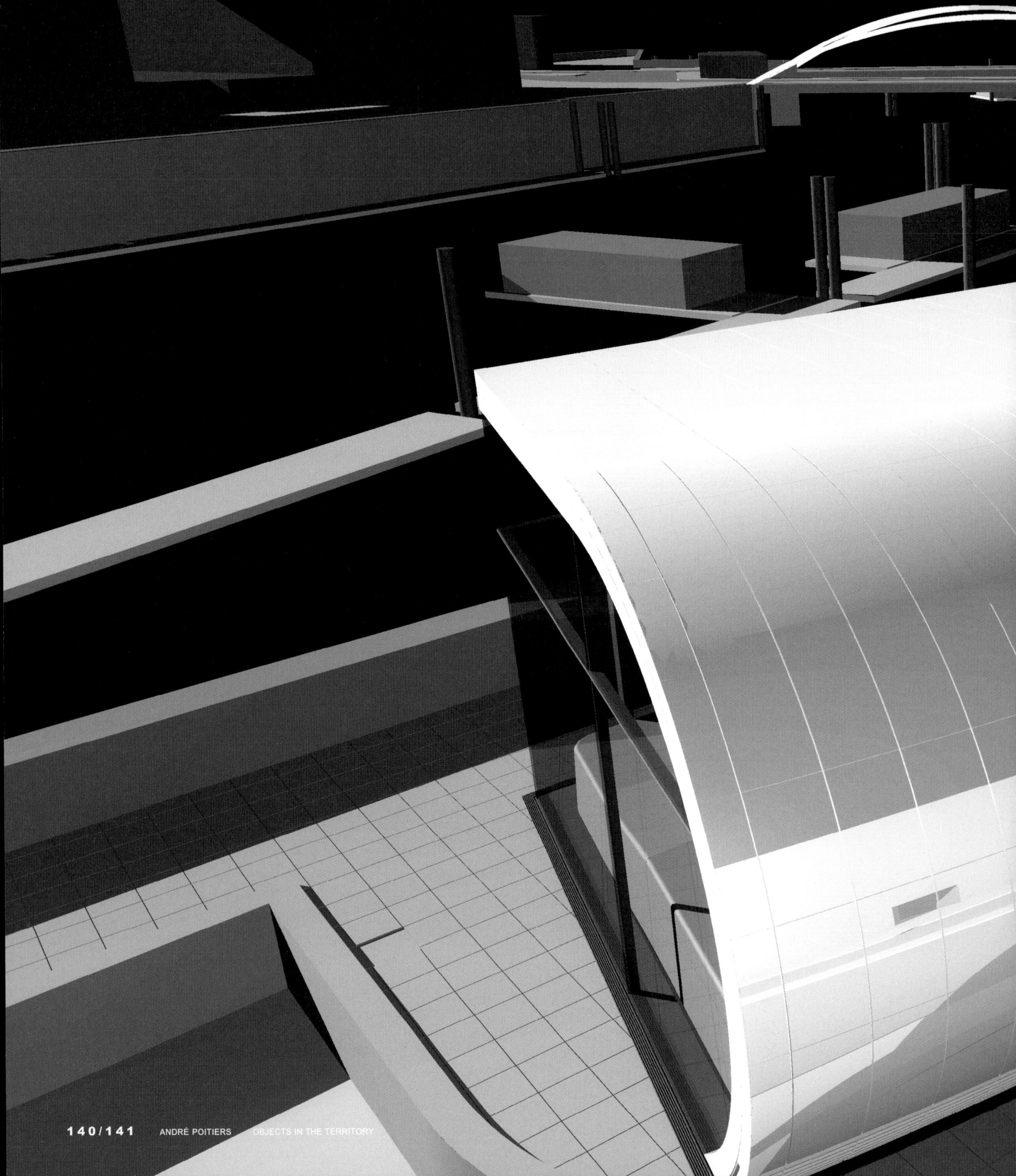

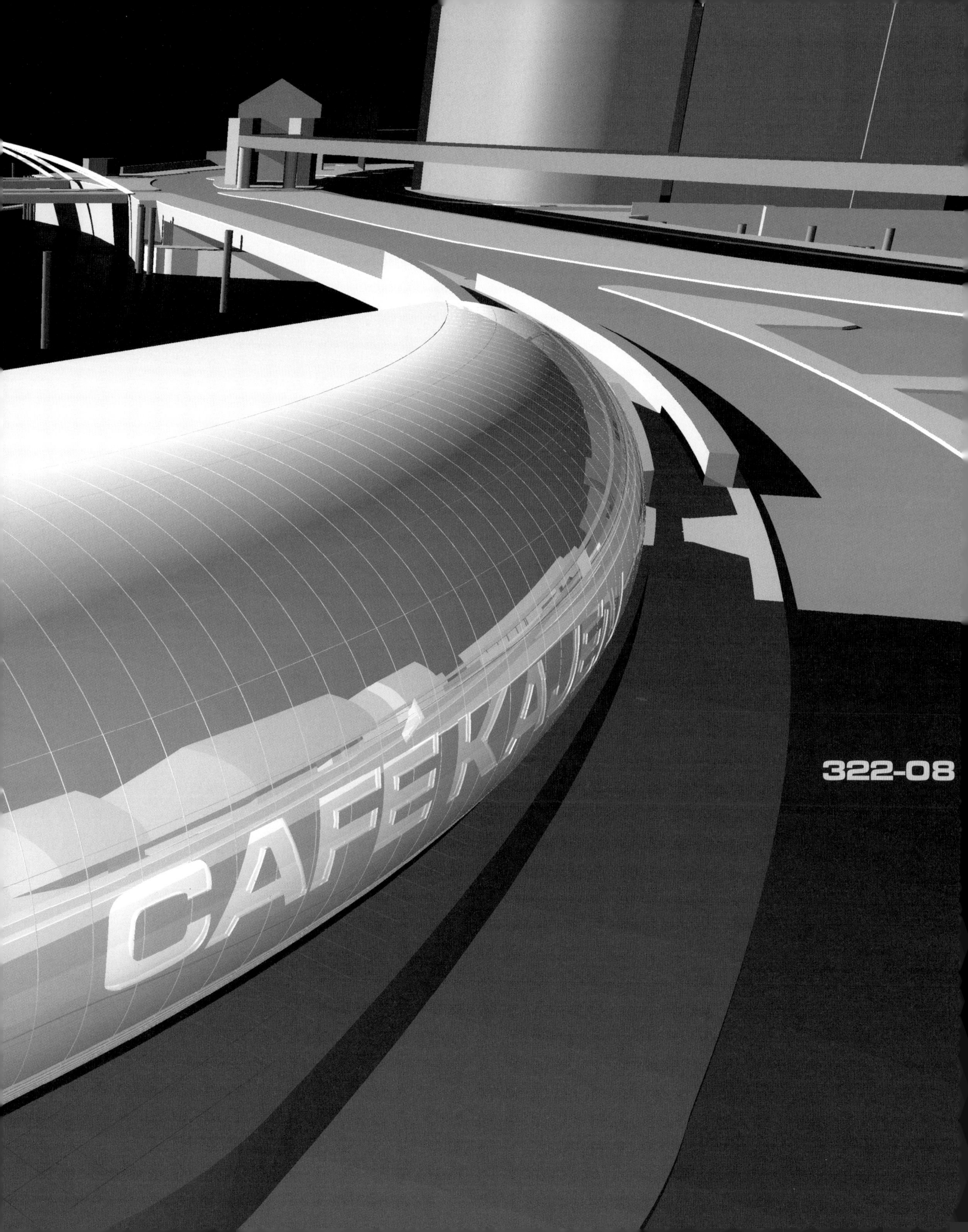
CAFÉKAJEN
322-08

321-09

OFFICE BUILDING / BONN / 2000

NEMOS HOUSE

321-09

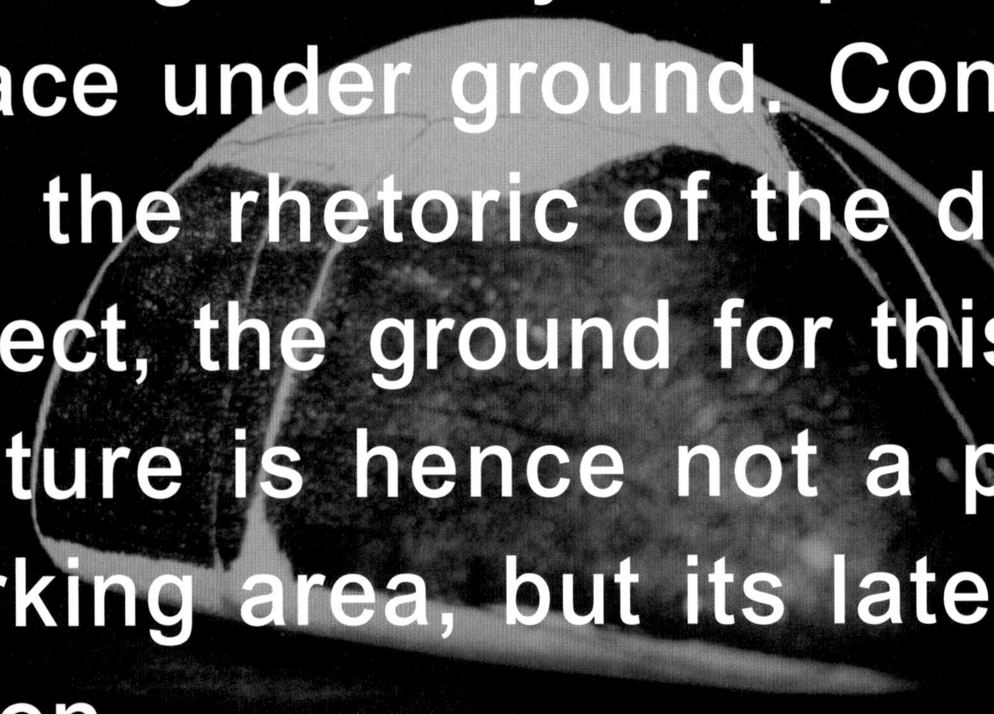

Masked by the mirror-smooth surface of its ground plate, the building invisibly occupies a lot of space under ground. Contradicting the rhetoric of the dropped object, the ground for this architecture is hence not a passive parking area, but its latent condition.

SECRETLY EMBEDDED

Rather like the Donut or the community centre, the Nemos House looks like one of Poitiers' Drop Buildings, placed on the ground like UFOs from outer space, unconnected with their location. If you take a close look at the digital renderings of the project, the site itself inevitably seems to be alienated when the alien object lands. The building itself is presented in photo-realistic detail, but the physical surroundings remain doggedly unreal. Schematically drawn roads and profiles of other buildings create an ambience whose synthetic charm is exceeded only by the pointed shapes of the digitally stunted trees.

The physical model suggests a rather more terrestrial atmosphere. The building and its surroundings now seem to be on a rather more equal footing, and rather more closely linked together, even though it is not easy to say how. It is significant that the building is surrounded by 8 lights on the ground here, rather like night lighting on helicopter landing pads, as though the site where the building has landed was selected for this purpose in advance. This territorial definition makes the location of the building seem less arbitrary. But the renderings do not make it clear whether the lights on the ground are anything more than a site decoration with a sci-fi theme. It is only the cross-section that shows that the ground lights represent the only way of knowing that the building occupies a lot of space underground. And so in reality the mirror-smooth surface containing the organically rounded building volume masks the fundamental way in which the building is totally tied up with its site. In contrast with the rhetoric of the dropped object, as suggested by the digital presentation of the building, the ground for this architecture is not a passive parking area, but its latent condition. But the building makes contradictory statements with its visible and invisible parts, as though it is deliberately trying to conceal its true identity.

This cat-and-mouse game with reality and simulation also dominates the volumetric design of the building. Given the forced stereometry of its cubature, here too everything seems to indicate that the building was developed independently of its context and came straight out of a drawer on to the site. But in fact the house is derived very directly from the set-back rules valid for the site: it draws back on its upper floors, so it can come closer to the neighbouring plots at ground level. And so purely in terms of building regulations it is a single-storey office building with two staggered floors, but with the difference that the backward movement is not hard and angular, but soft and rounded.

THE BUILDING IN ITS CONTEXT

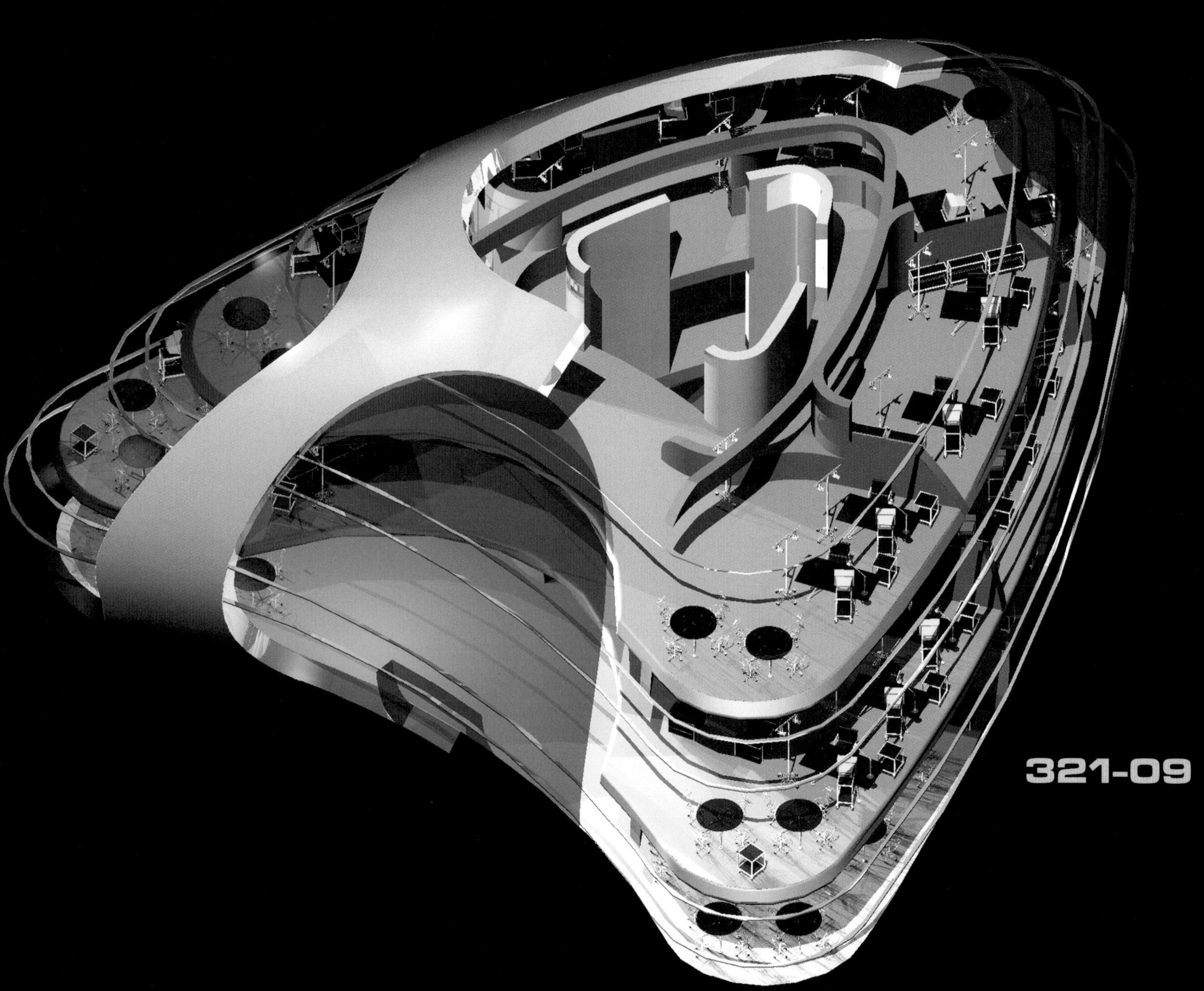

321-09

ISOMETRIC VIEW OF THE BUILDING

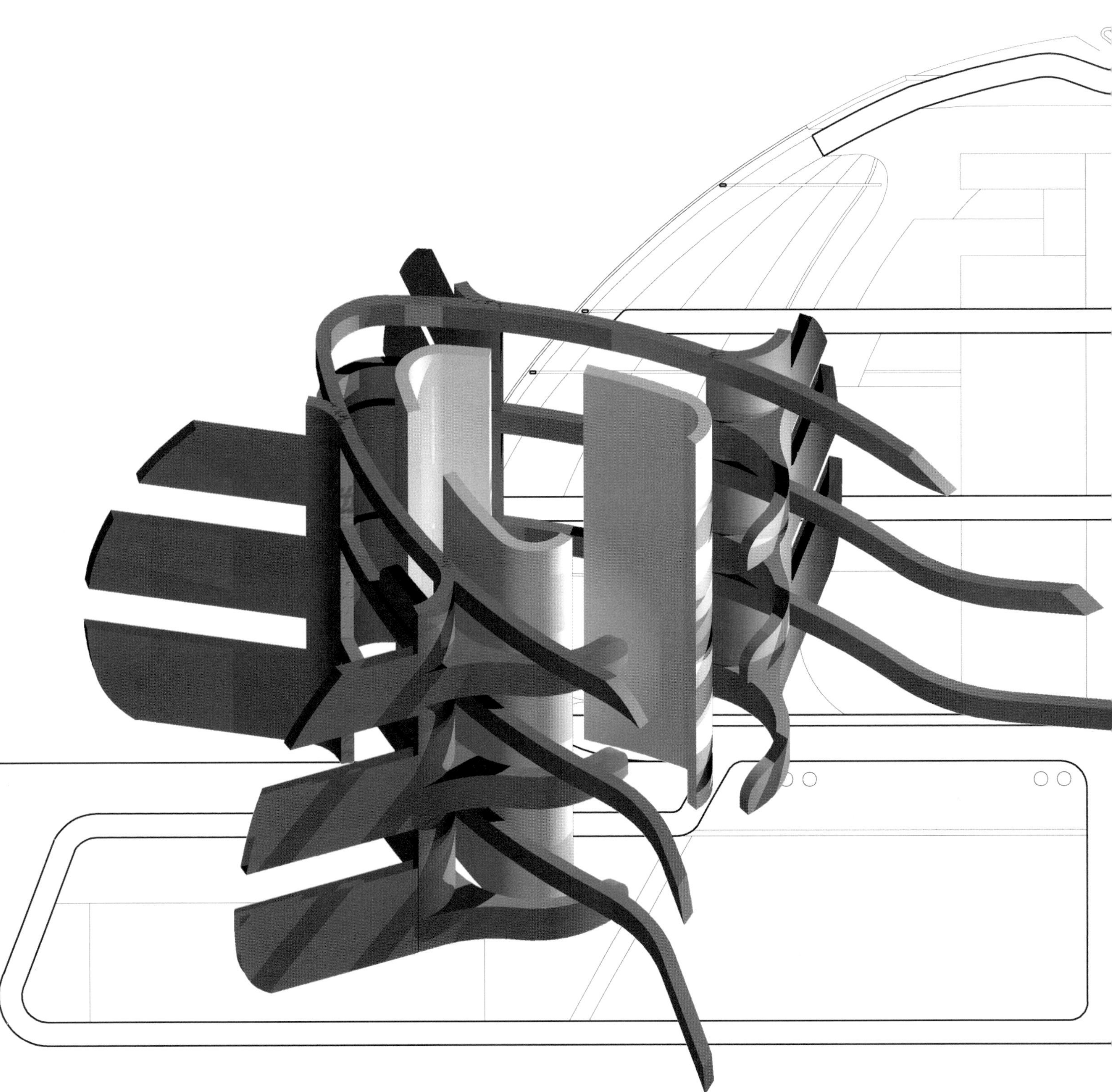

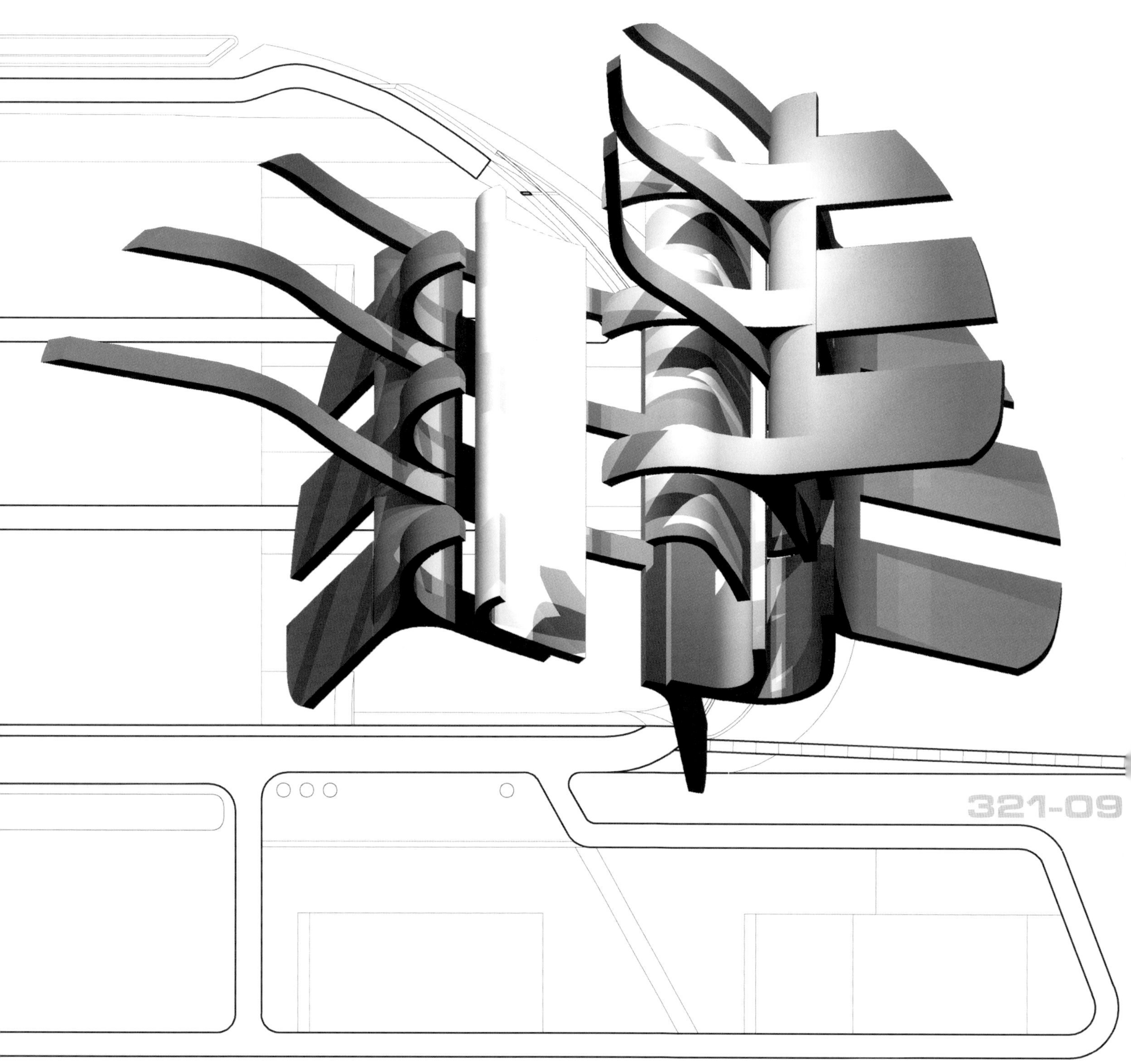

INTERNAL SPATIAL STRUCTURE AND LONGITUDINAL SECTION THROUGH THE BUILDING

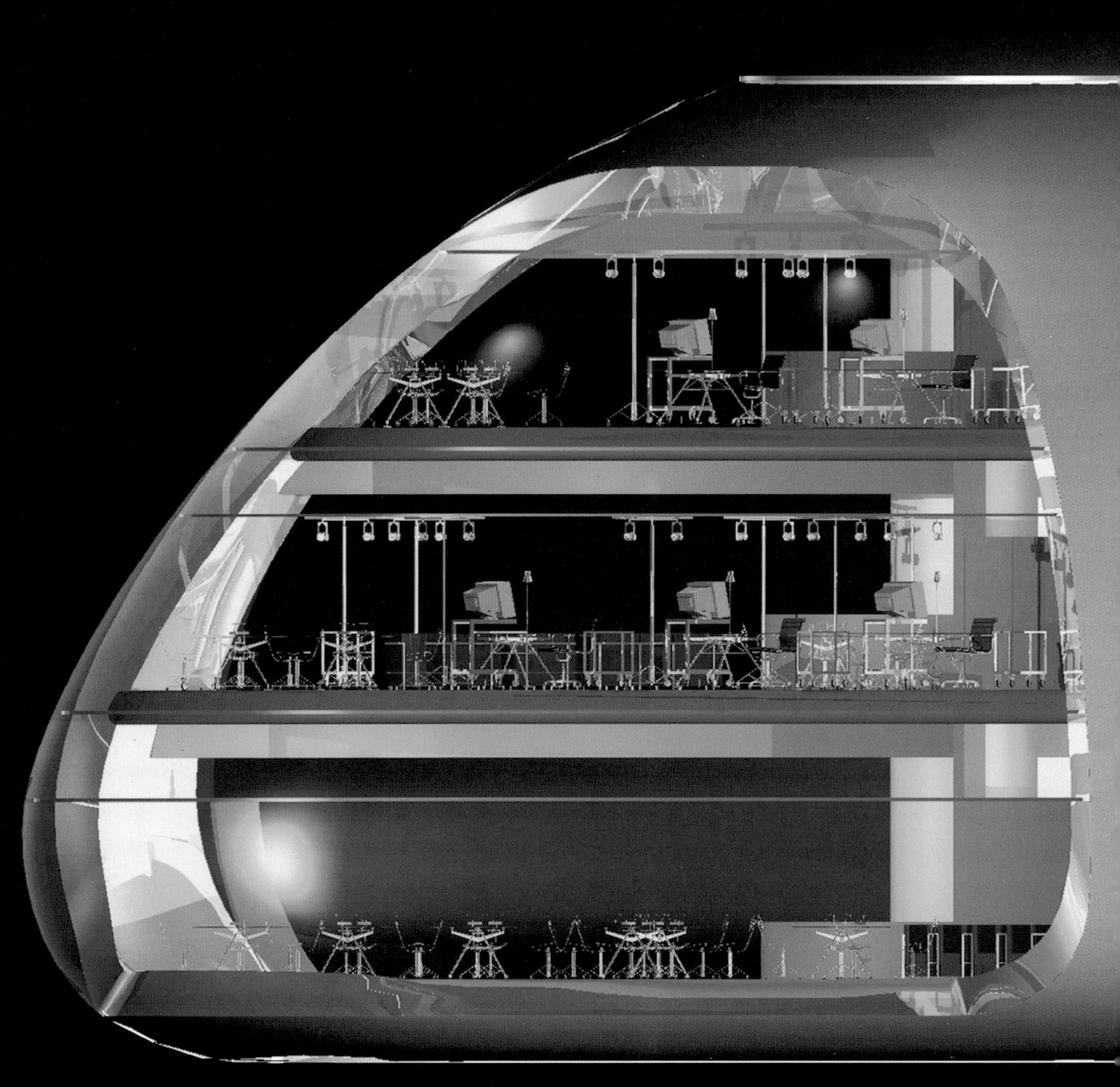

321-09

351-10

OFFICE BUILDING / BONN / 2001

BLIP

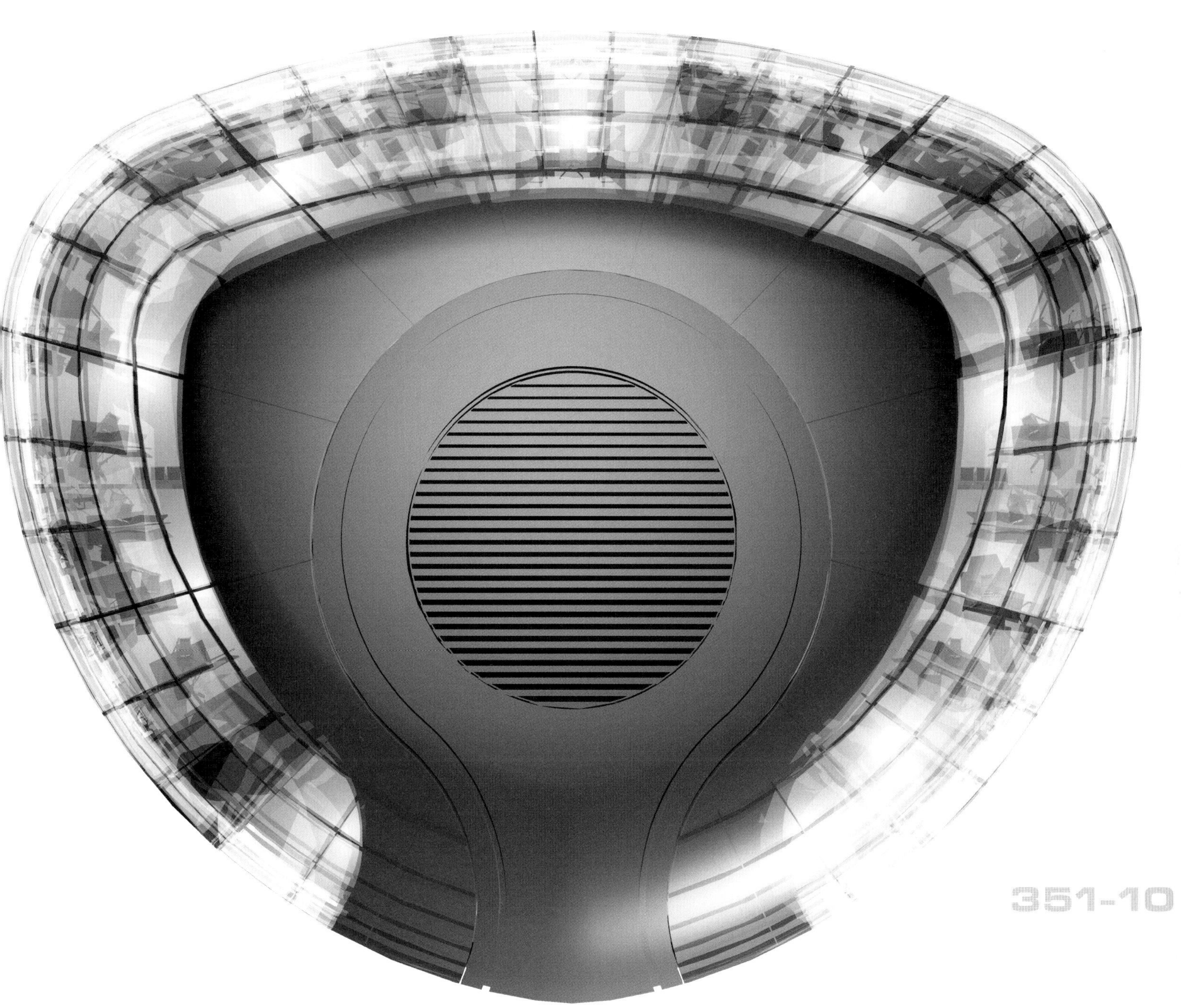

351-10

Floating above the roundabout like a traffic surveillance tower, the building gives the fluid space a double orientation: its body draws it towards the city, but the glazed offices tend to address the motorway.

TRAFFIC BLASTER

The starting-point for this project is a plot that was never intended for development – the land inside a traffic roundabout. But even though the place is essentially a waste product of transport planning, it does have a specific urban function: placed directly on the motorway exit, it gives visitors arriving by car their first sense of the town and works like a town gate. But this boundary is no longer architectural, as it used to be until the early 19th century; what happens instead is that people start to drive differently as they adapt their speed to that imposed by the roundabout.

Occupying this amorphous location with architecture is a tricky business. Suburbia does not like being urbanized, it is no longer subordinated to the city, not sub-urbia, but "Zwischenstadt" (Thomas Sieverts), intermediate city: a space without a centre of gravity, an extent without a direction, but still full of currents and movements. Given the specific context, this roundabout acquires the significance of a "suburban square". In an urban square, space in its scale, perception and function is mainly defined by the pedestrians, but here the car takes over this defining role. This automobile logic also defines the architectural scope of the "Blib". And this begins with access: because the circular traffic effectively closes the island off with a wall of movement, the building can only be reached via underground passages.

But is it a building at all? The "Blib" floats above the square like a traffic surveillance tower. The ground beneath it rises slightly from the level, forming a kind of "Infra-Lobby" for the offices above. The building is placed off-centre in the square, thus giving the fluid space a double orientation: its body draws it towards the city, but the glazed offices tend to address the motorway. But even the apparently amorphous volume itself features an internal hierarchy owing to its conceptual origins from a virtual CD player from a MTV spot. Its structural principle – a CD drive and cover held together by a linking section at the back – can be discerned in the support structure and layout of the "Blib", and also gives it a top and a bottom, a front and a back. And just like the CD player, the "Blib's" information is fed in from the front – the traffic flow animates and informs its internal and external life. By working directly with the physical parameters of its context in this way, the "Blib" does not exploit its periphery in purely functional terms, as an office park, but addresses it as a genuine part of the "cityscape" that is increasingly leaving the town far behind as a model.

351-10

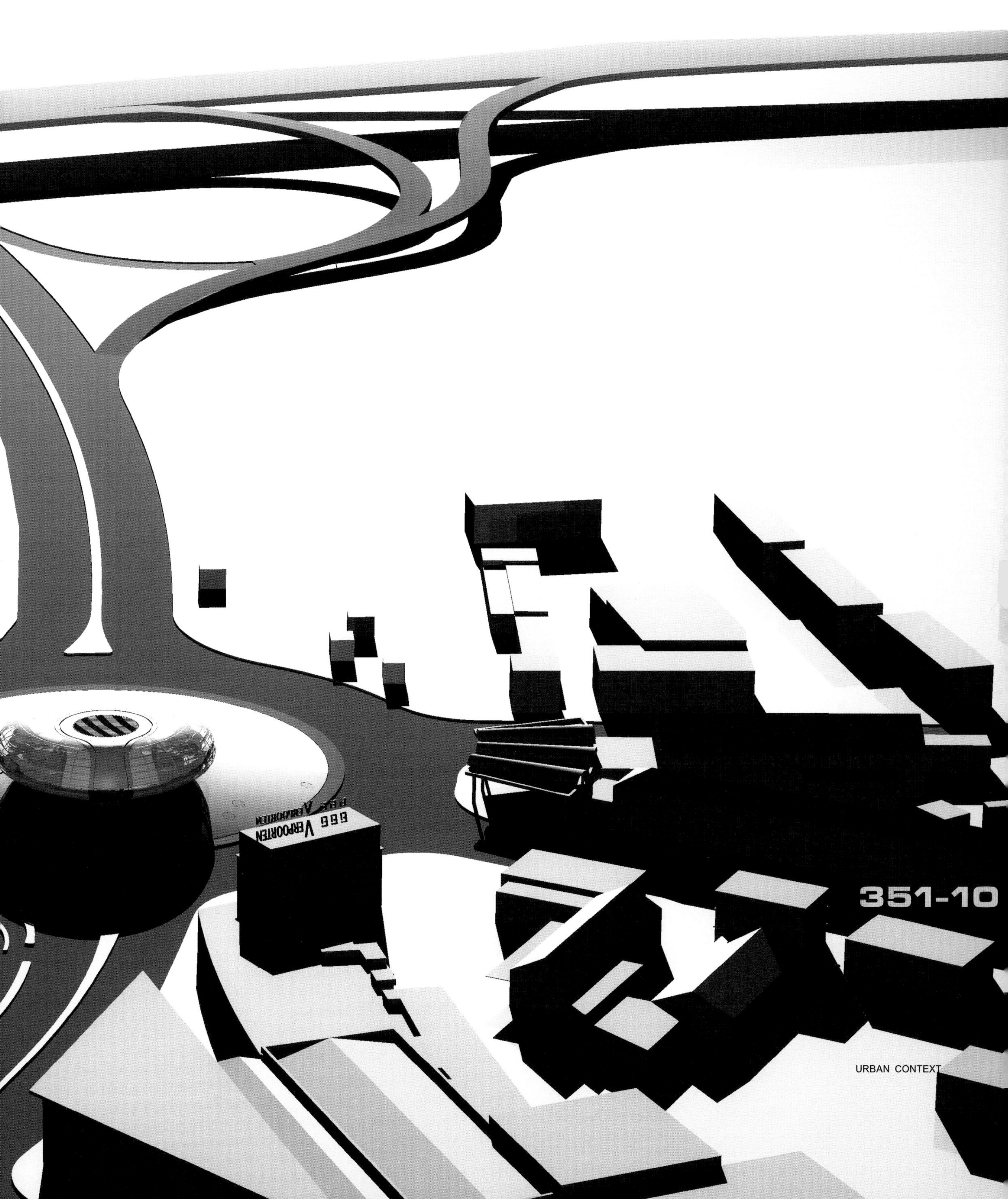

351-10

URBAN CONTEXT

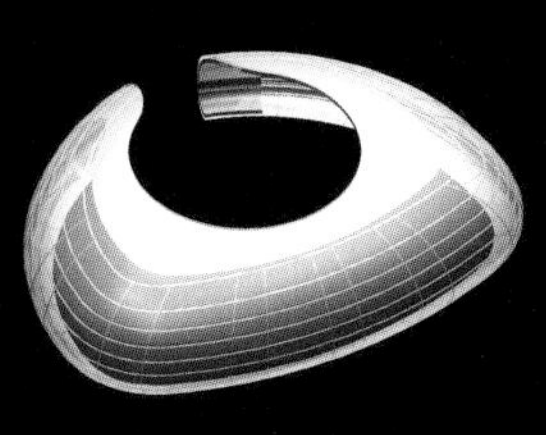
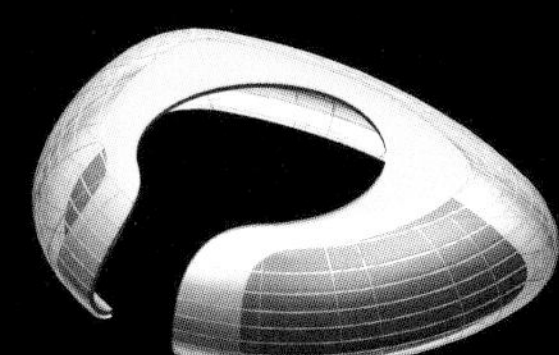
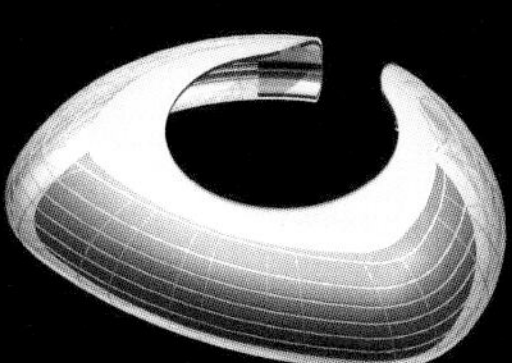
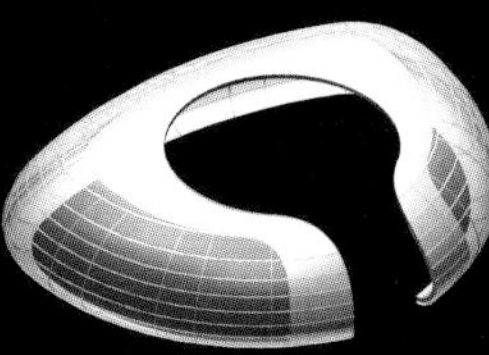
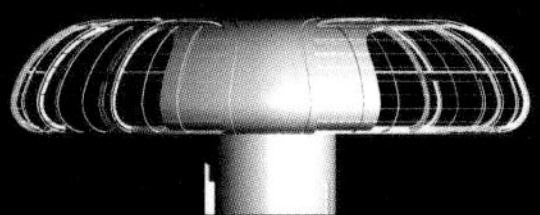

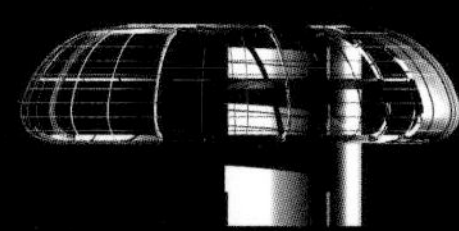
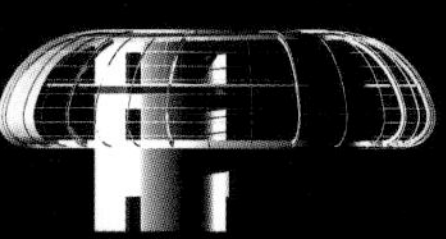

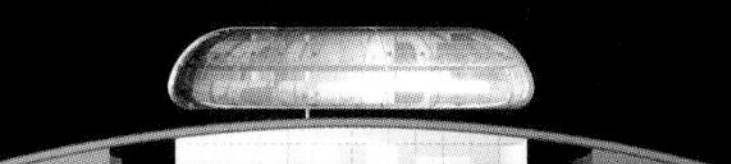

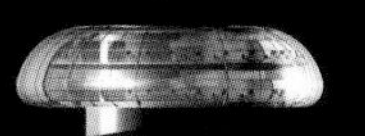

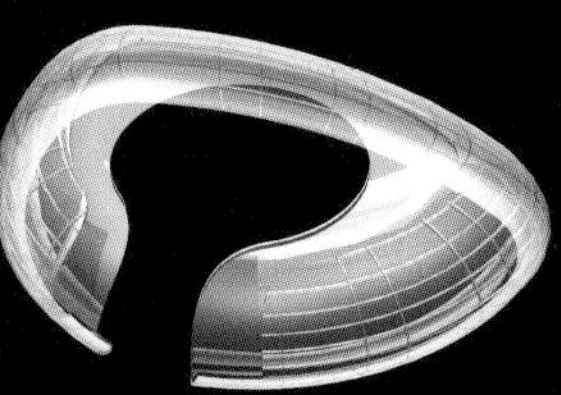
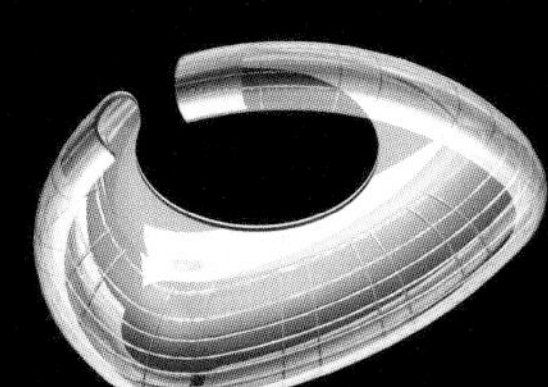
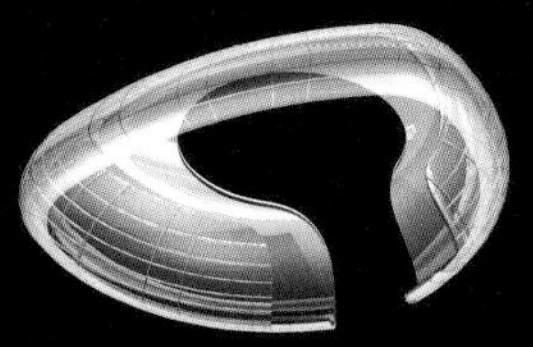
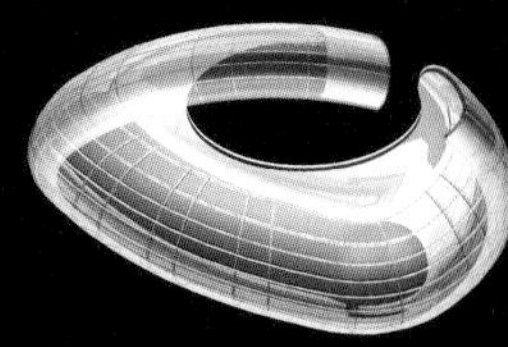
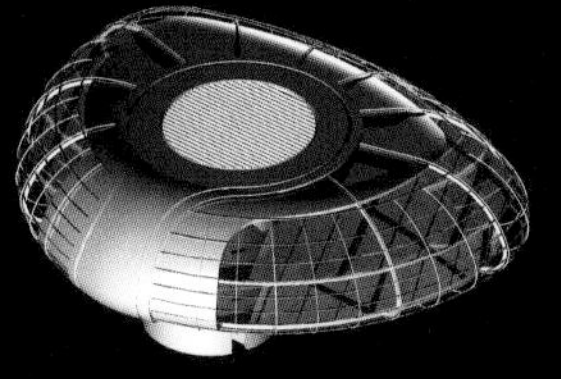
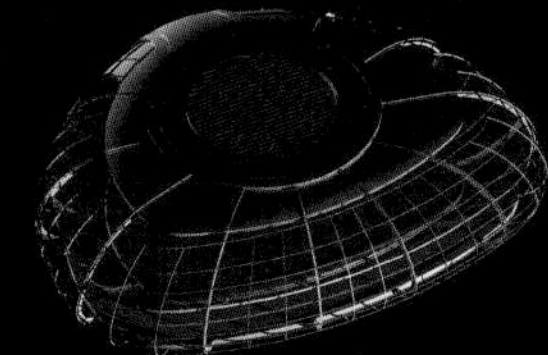
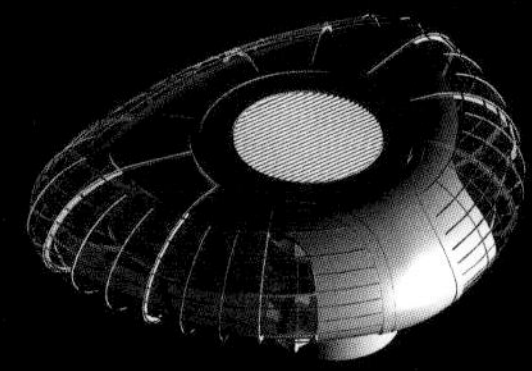
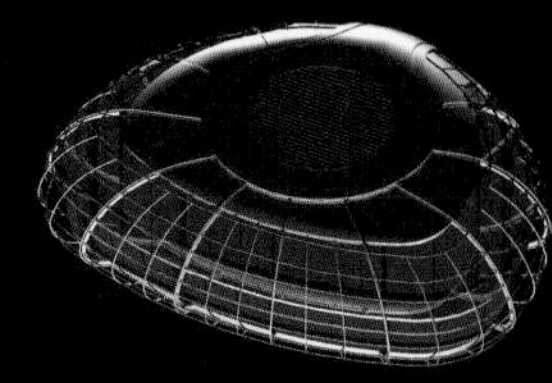
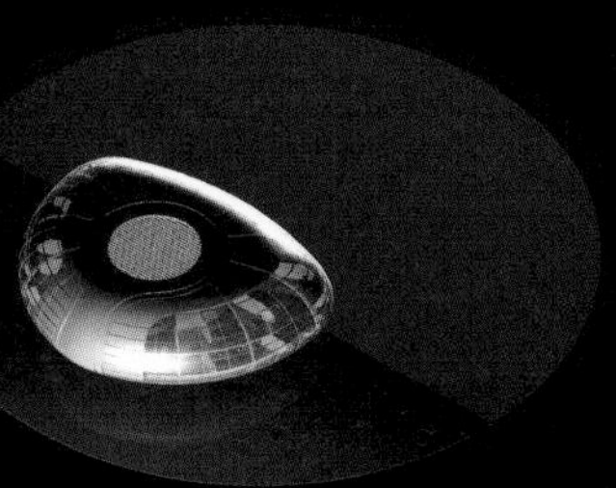

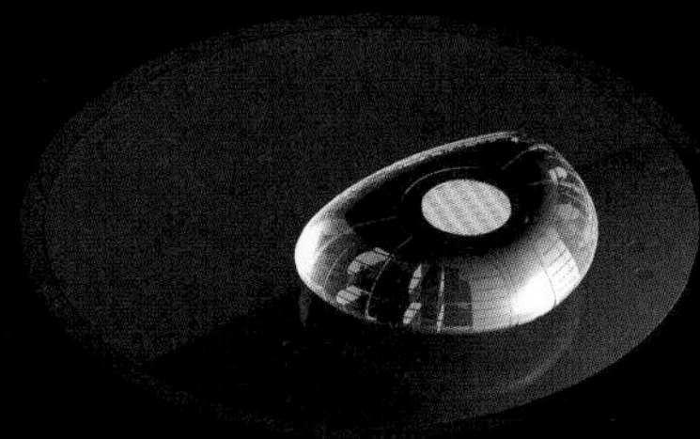
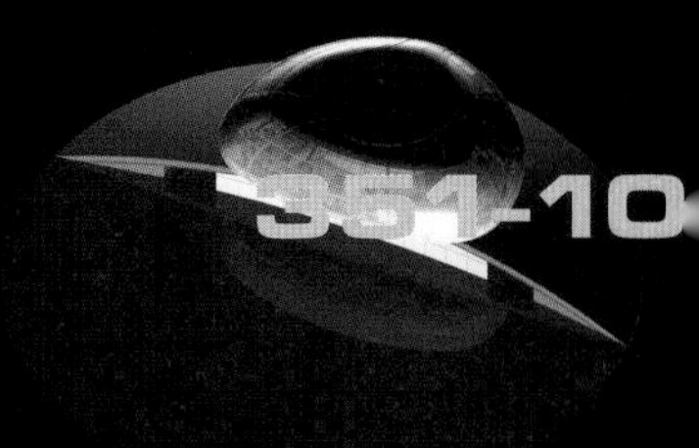

VIEWS OF THE BUILDING AND ITS SECTIONS
(STRUCTURE, ENVELOPE, CORE, SURROUNDINGS)

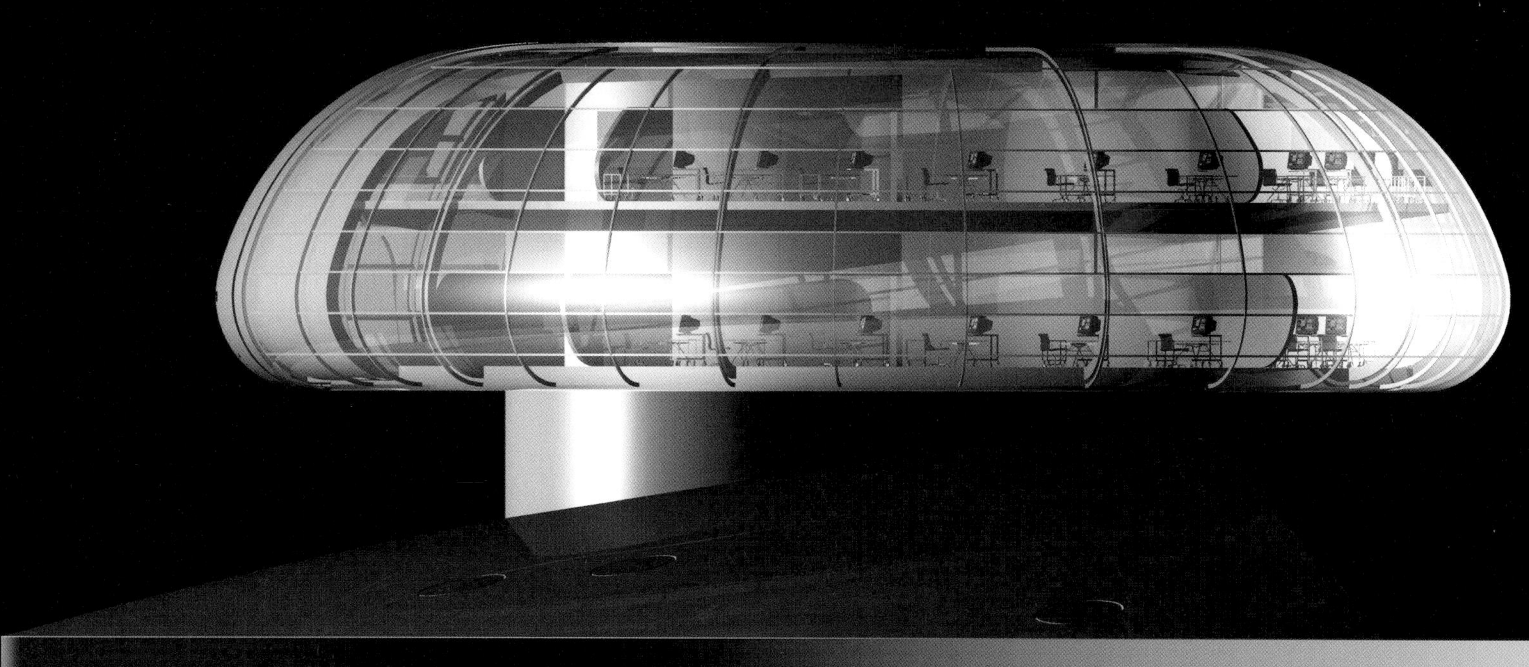

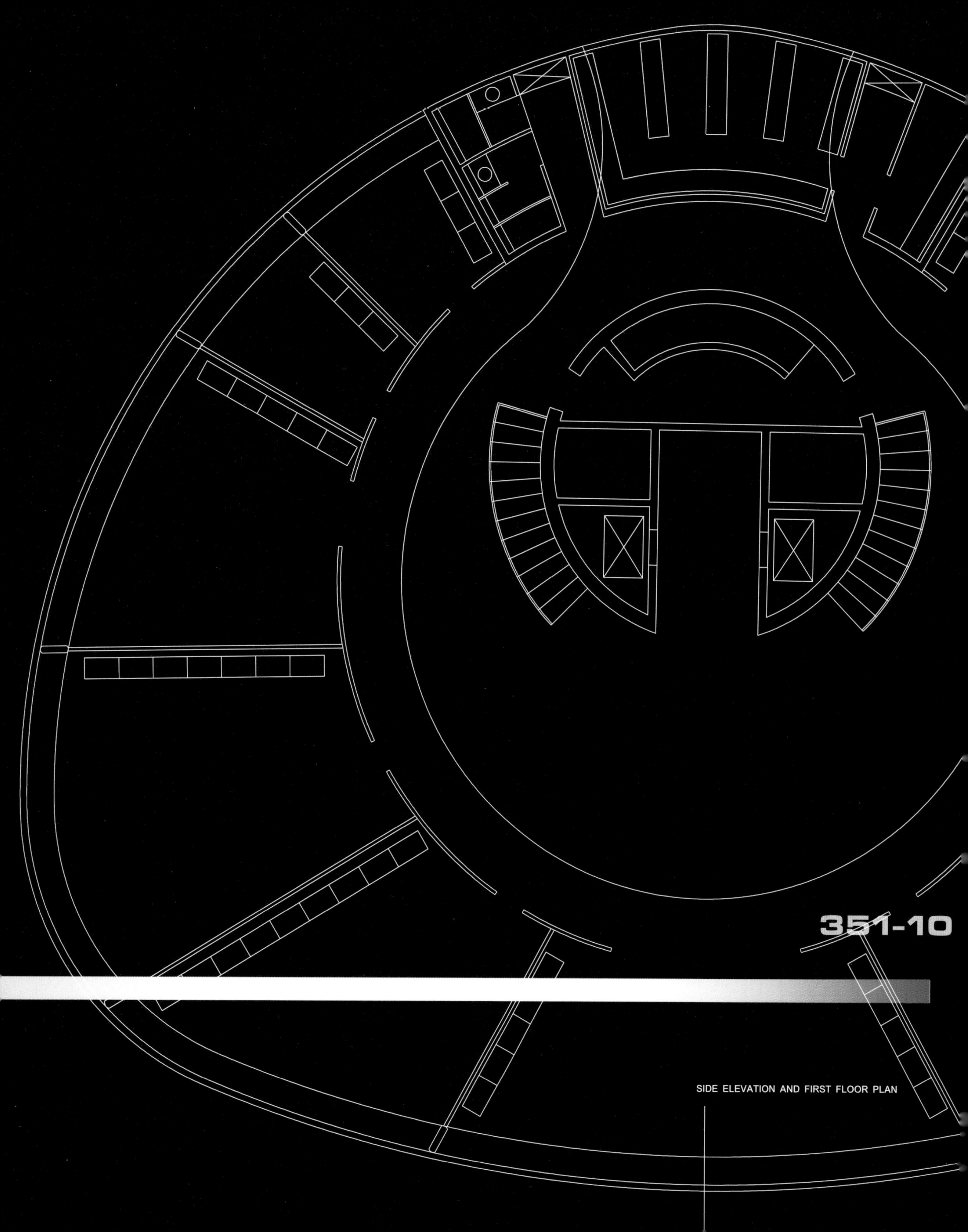

SIDE ELEVATION AND FIRST FLOOR PLAN

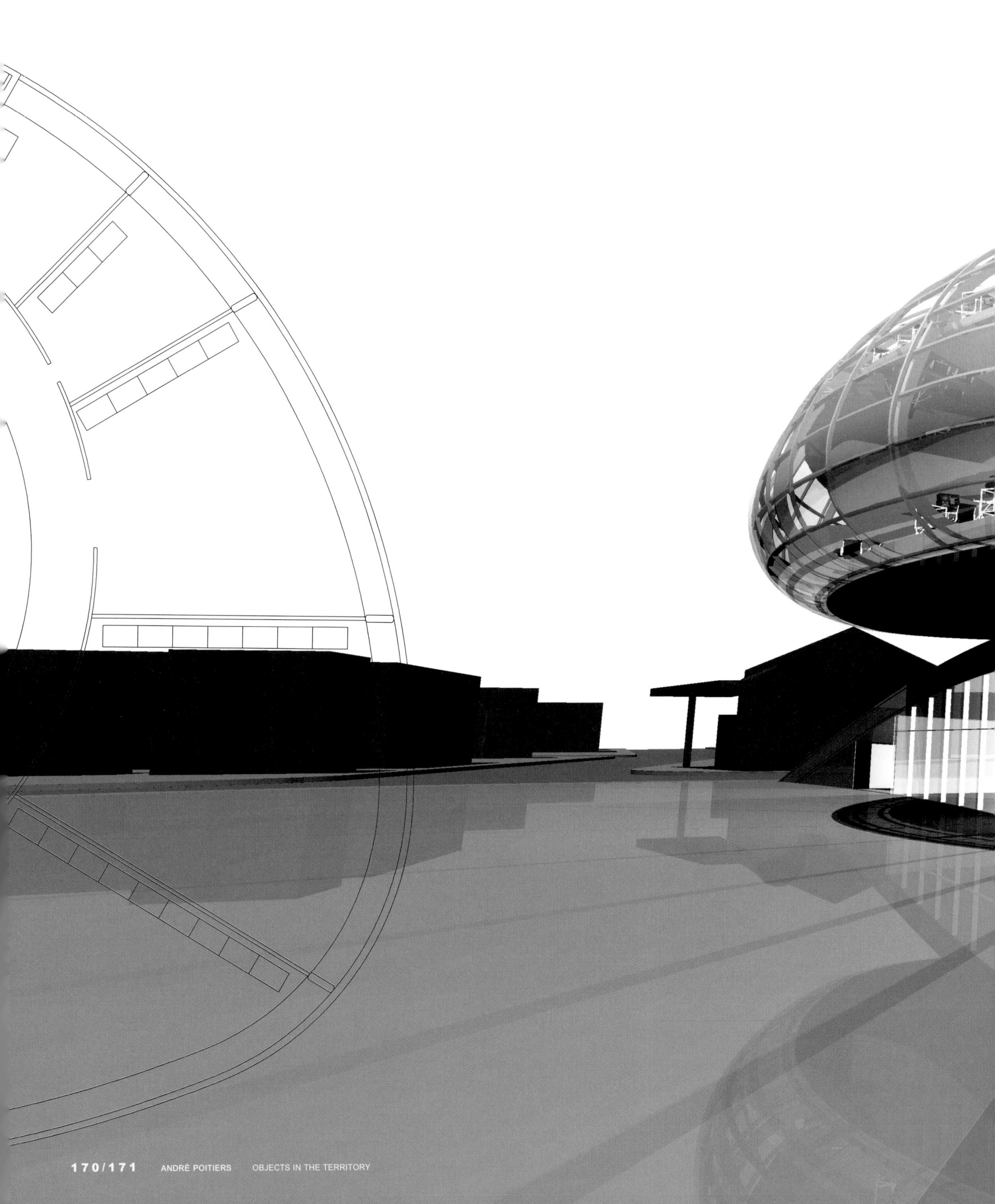

351-10

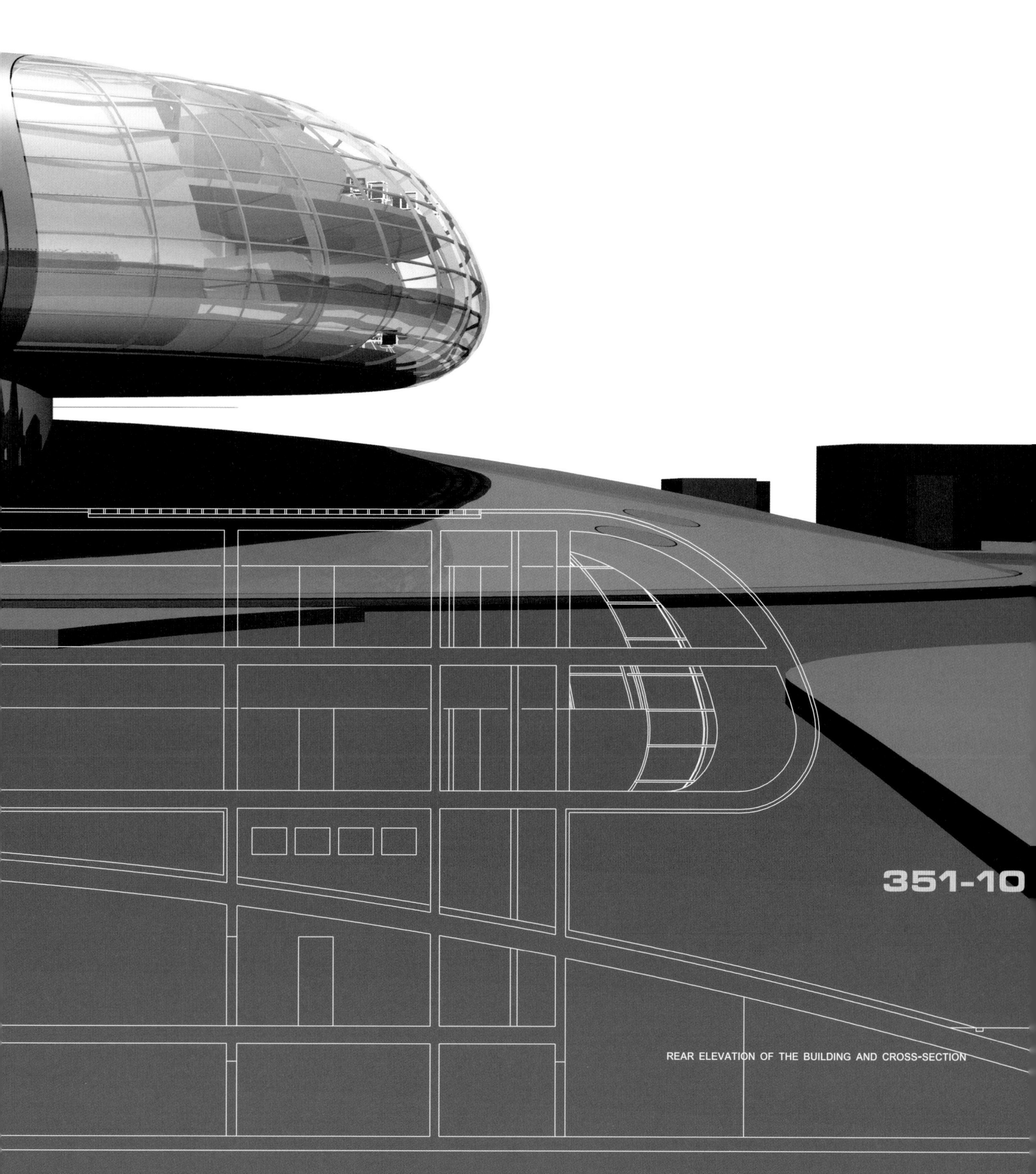

REAR ELEVATION OF THE BUILDING AND CROSS-SECTION

705-11

2001

CAST HOUSE

705-11

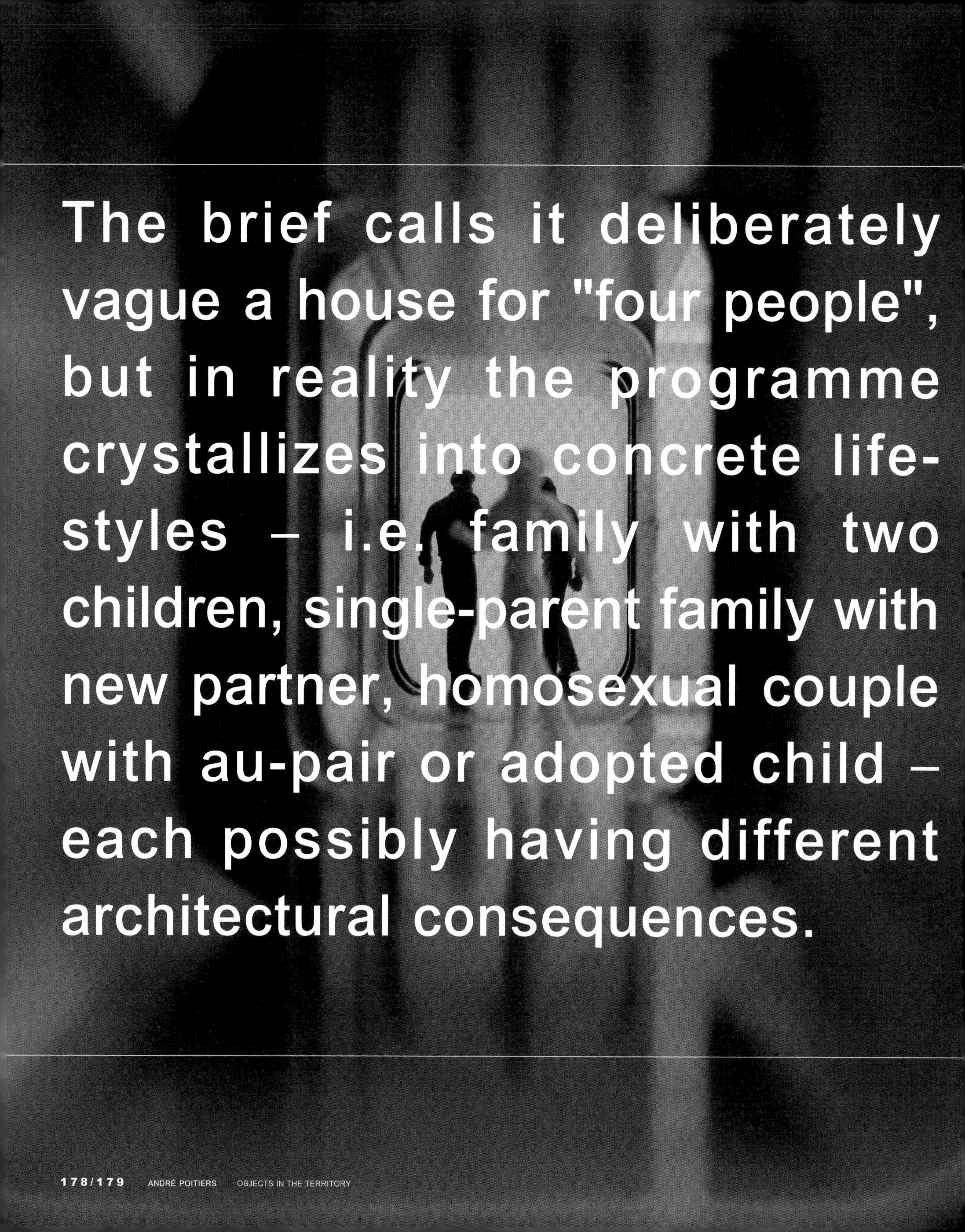

The brief calls it deliberately vague a house for "four people", but in reality the programme crystallizes into concrete life-styles – i.e. family with two children, single-parent family with new partner, homosexual couple with au-pair or adopted child – each possibly having different architectural consequences.

A HOUSE TO BECOME

In spring 2001 the SZ-Magazin, the magazine supplement to the Süddeutsche Zeitung, announced a restricted competition for the "Contemporary House". They were looking for "a house for four people, in Central Europe, with 200 square metres of usable space on a flat site of about 500 square metres", which was not to cost more that DM 500,000. The Cast House interprets this brief, which is at the same time both general and specific, by using an organizational principle for housing that was defined by the Californian Case Study Houses 50 years ago: the living space is laid out in a single-storey building that is divided into a public and a private area by a patio. The whole design for the Cast House is developed from this zoning decision. The private area includes three bedrooms and a bathroom; the kitchen, living- and dining-rooms make up the public sphere of the house. The entrance and the patio set in between form a buffer zone that both divides and connects the two parts of the house.

Instead of a finished building, the design presents a spatially rendered diagram that contains a variety of genetic information in the manner of a genotype, and this can be made into a house by further developing various phenotypes. It is only in this process that the house prototype is customized to become an architectural product by applying internal and external parameters. The brief deliberately keeps things vague by saying "four people", but in reality the structure of the residences crystallizes into concrete life-styles – family with two children, single-parent family with new partner, homosexual couple with au-pair or adopted child, several different parties sharing etc. – all of which can have very different architectural consequences. And the brief also does not stipulate that the "contemporary house" has only to be a dwelling. Because it is organized in two halves, a childless couple could live and work in the house at the same time. In this case what was formerly the private section would be changed into a workroom, while everyday life would be entirely in what was originally defined as the public living area. The wide-ranging scope of this development process is shown by the fact that this reprogramming of the architecture completely reverses the original coding of public and private spaces. The office now becomes the public part of the house, and the living area mutates into a private domain.

The architecture would be transformed in just the same way as soon as external local parameters like price or the shape of the plot are applied to the prototype. Does the land surround the house on all sides, with ample space between it and its neighbours, or is the site so narrow and deep that it would be completely filled up by the house? The first case would correspond with the detached house, and the second with the terraced house – house typologies, in other words, that create different neighbourly relations between the occupants at the next stage. Similarly, consequences would follow from extending the house, laterally or upwards, and this would be entirely possible given its modular construction. The special quality of this house lies in the fact that its final definition is fluid: a prototype is defined by an initial decision, and that prototype is as concrete as necessary and as open as possible.

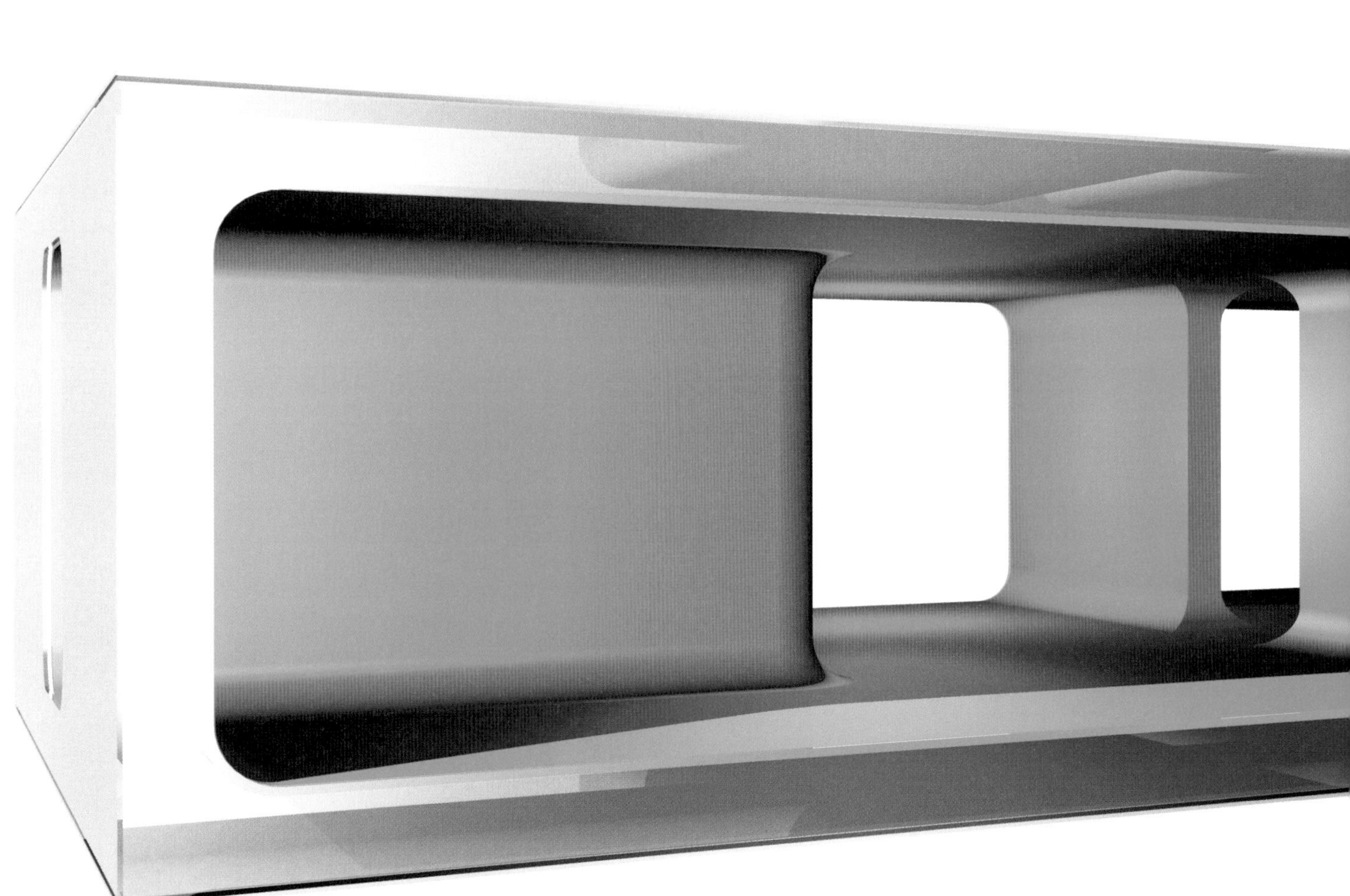

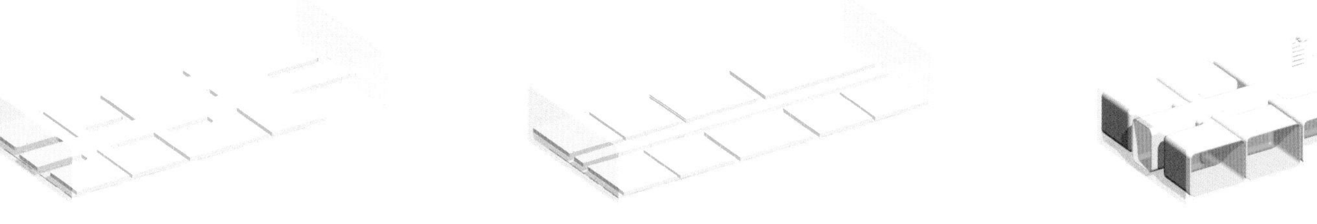

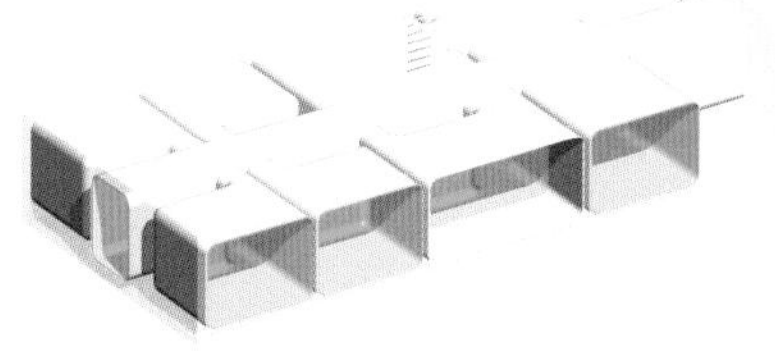

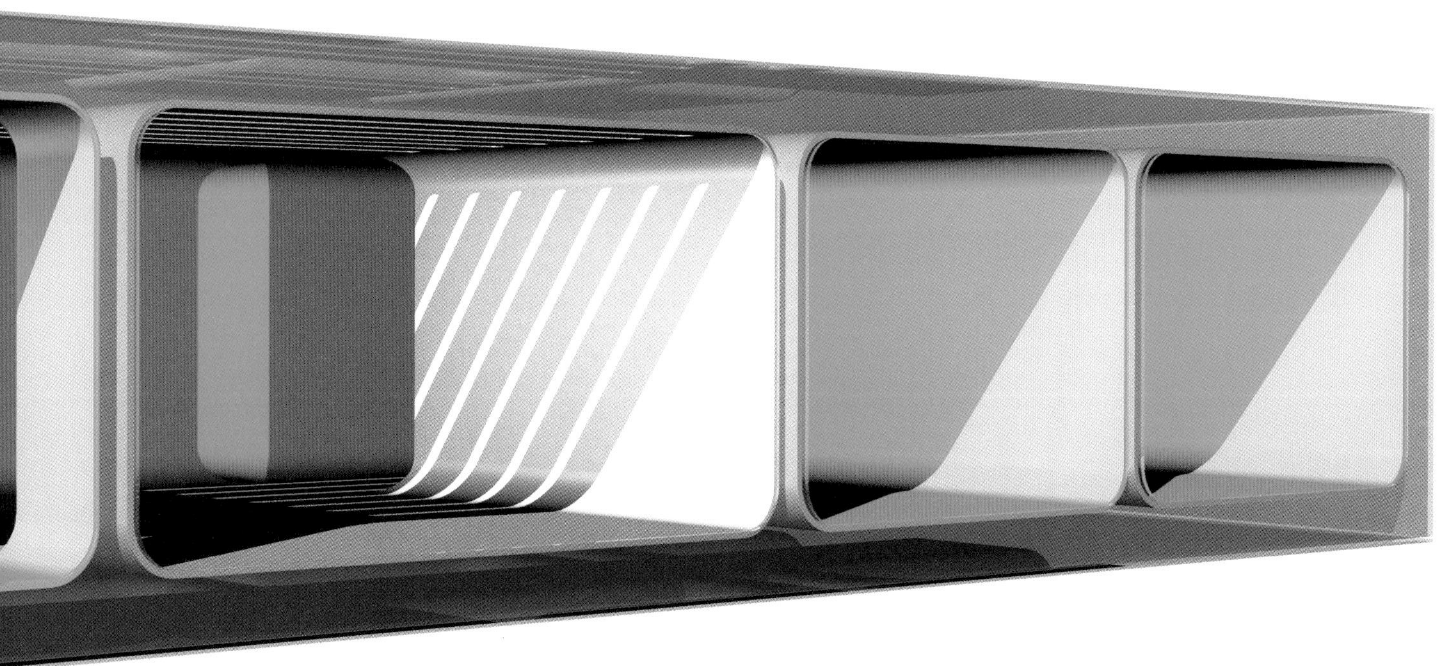

705-11

PERSPECTIVE OF THE BUILDING AND DEVELOPMENT OF THE SPATIAL CONCEPT

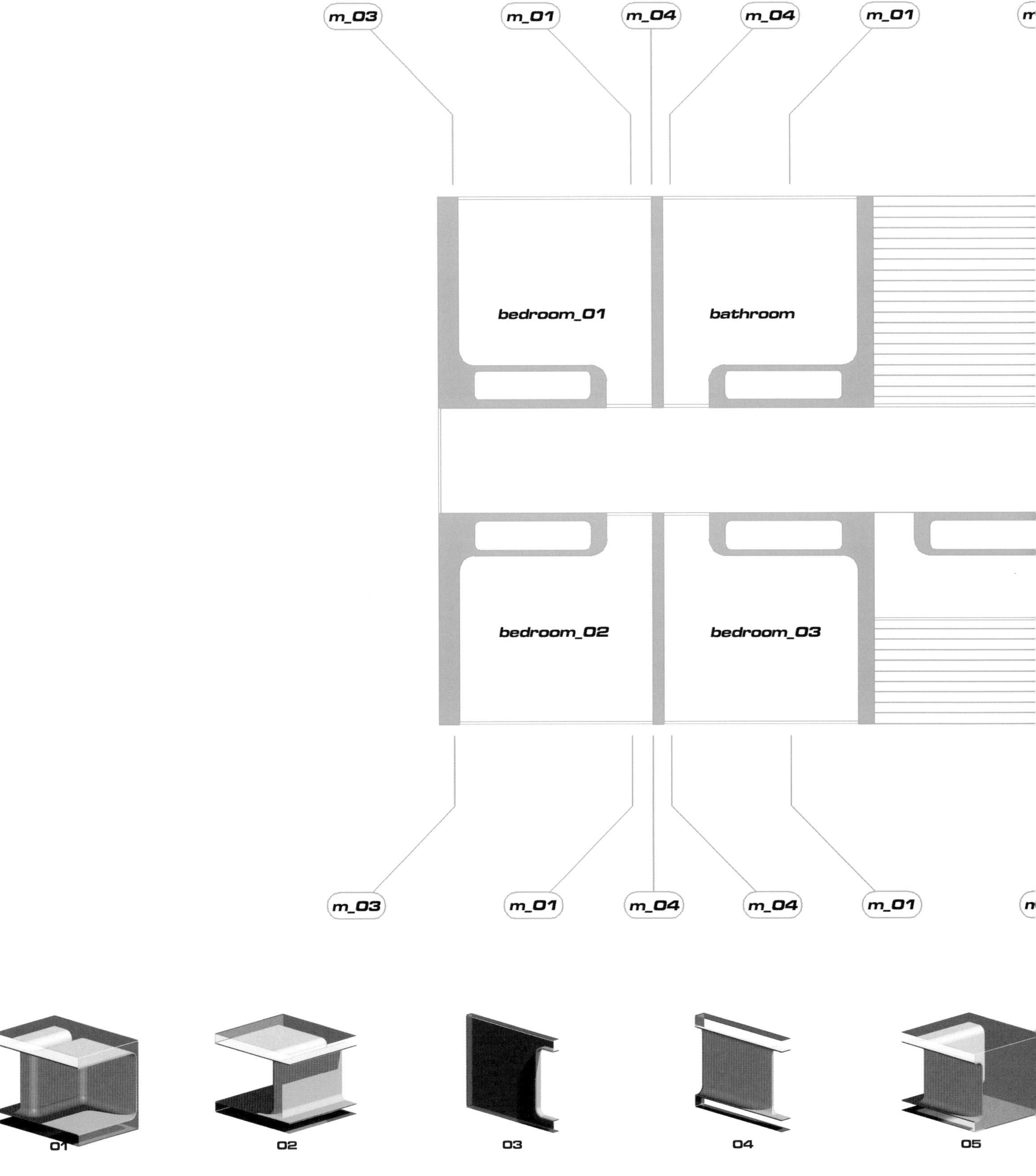

m_03
m_01
m_04
m_04
m_01
bedroom_01
bathroom
bedroom_02
bedroom_03
m_03
m_01
m_04
m_04
m_01
01
02
03
04
05

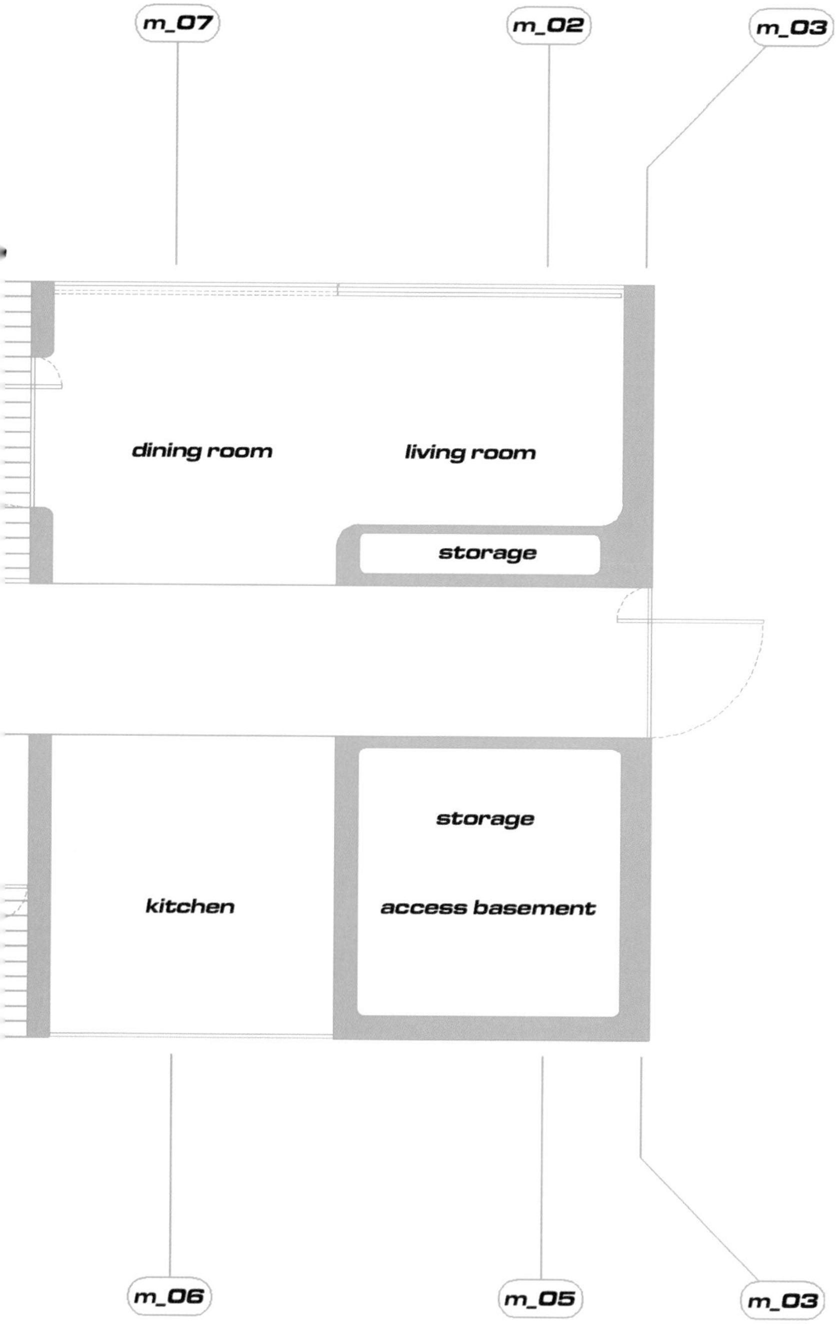

m_07
m_02
m_03

dining room
living room
storage

storage
kitchen
access basement

m_06
m_05
m_03

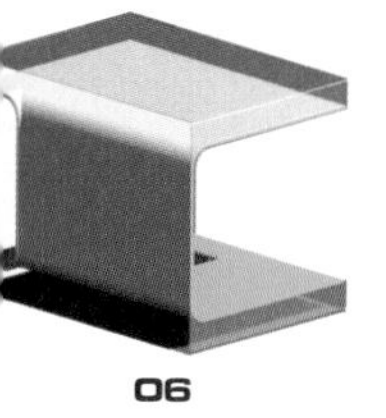
06

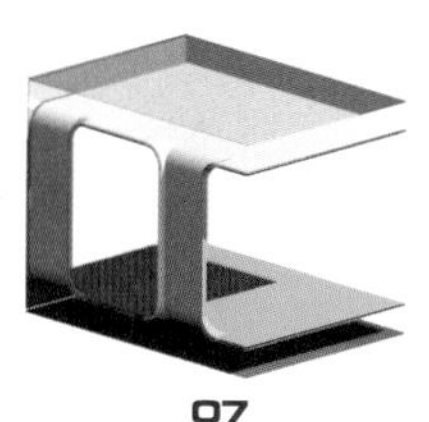
07

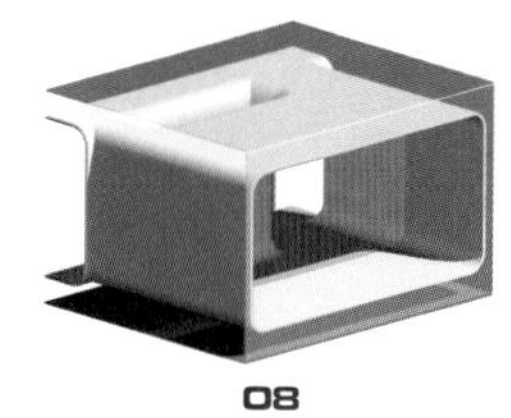
08

09

705-11

GROUND PLAN AND BUILDING MODULES

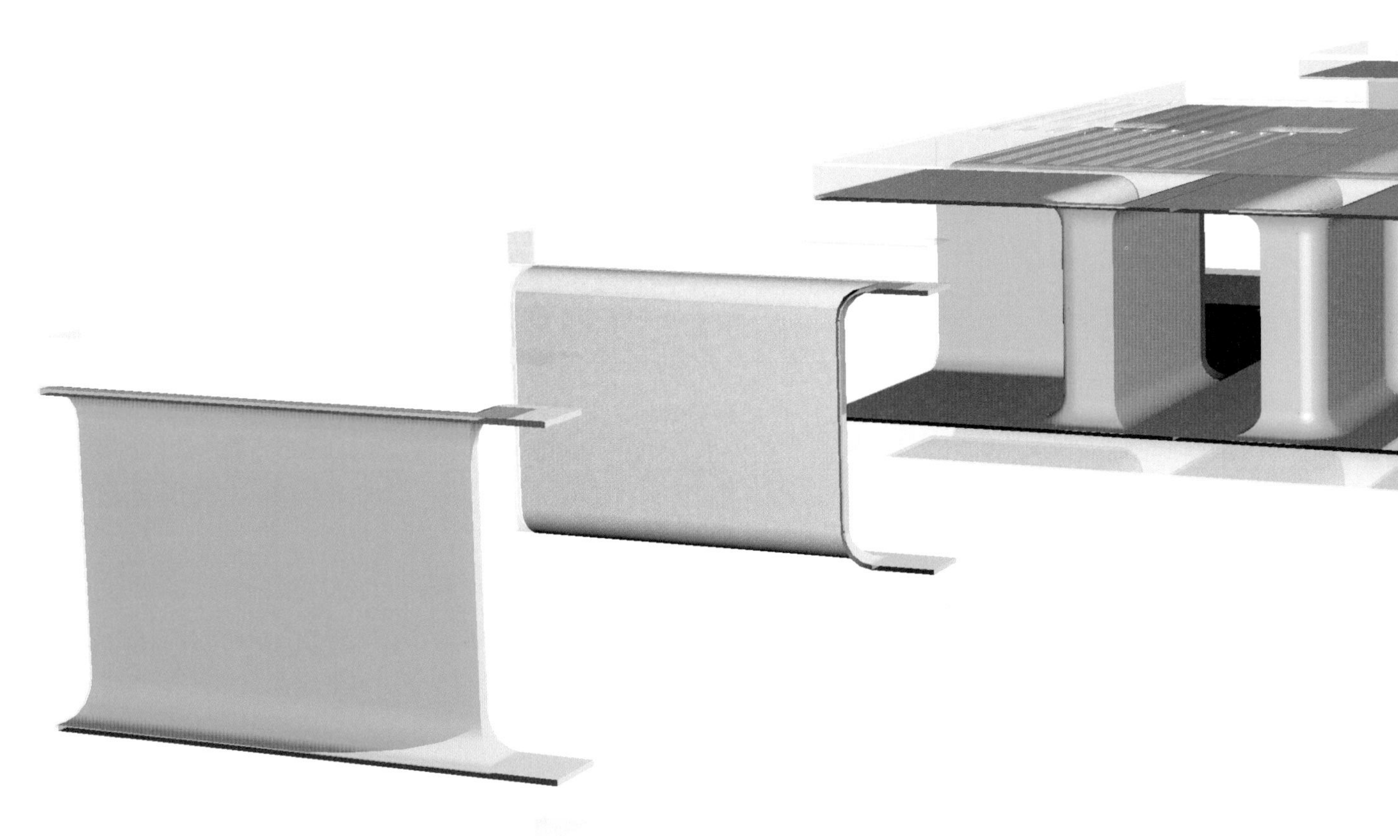

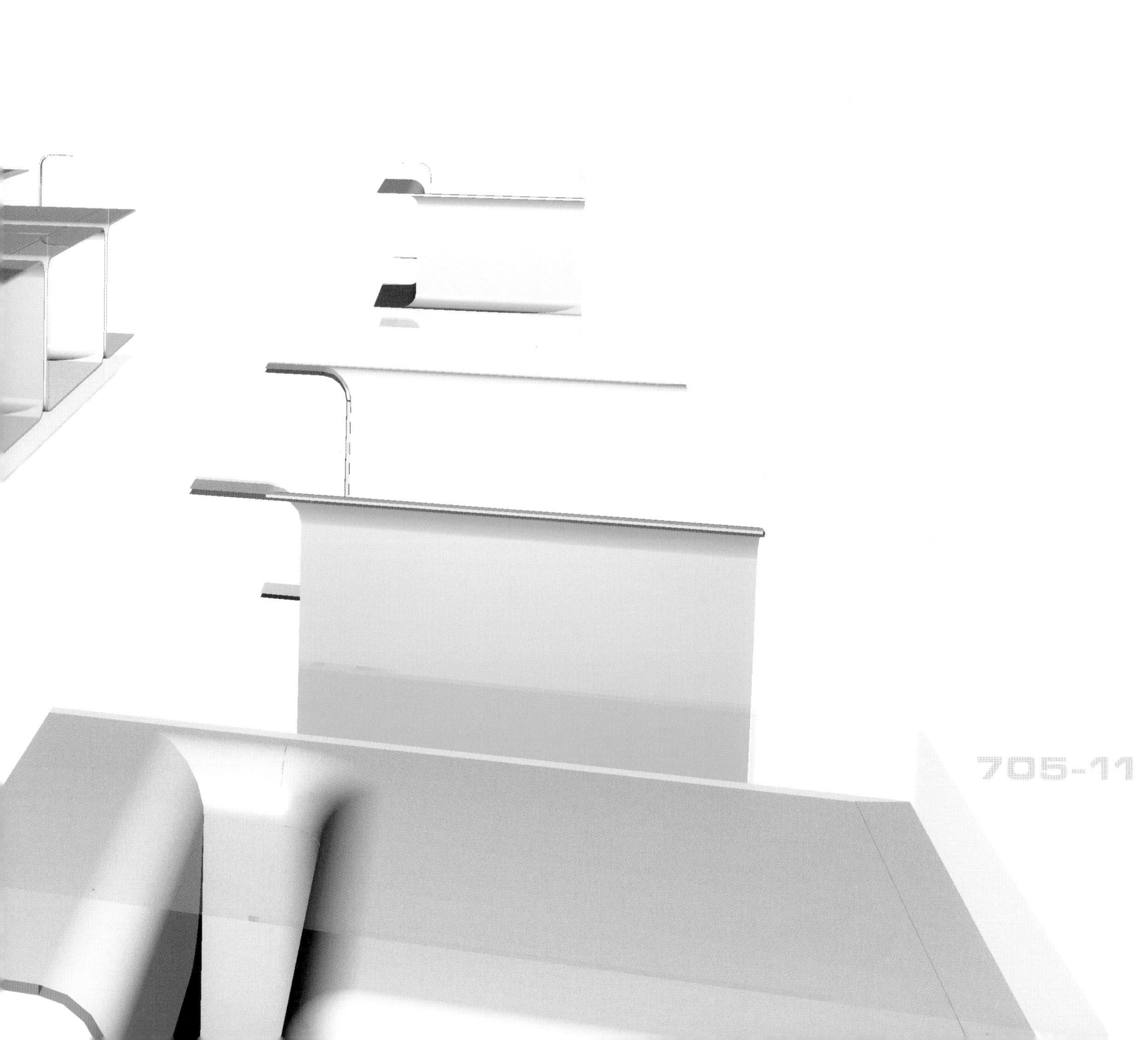
705-11

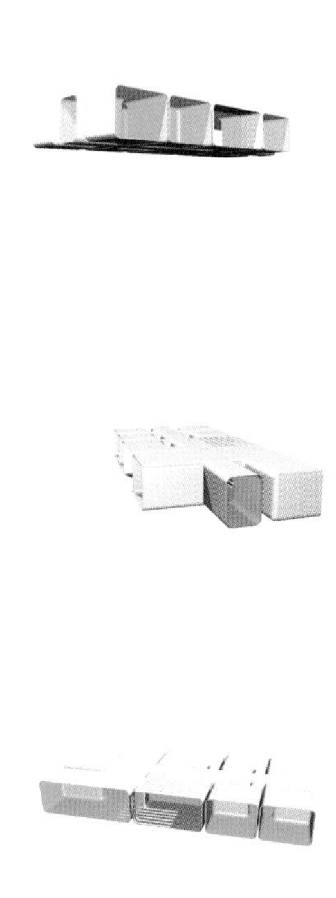

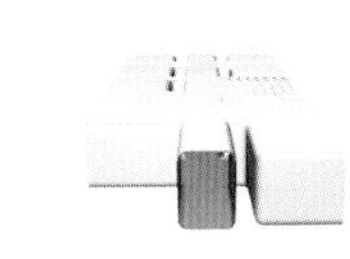
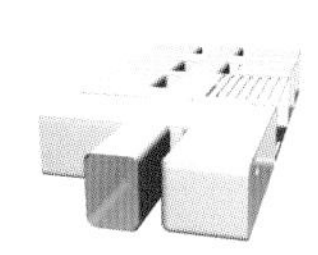
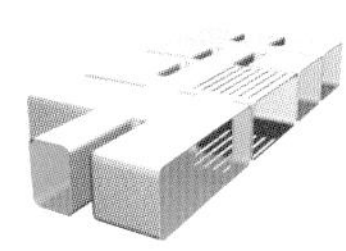

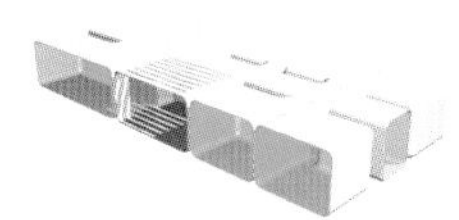
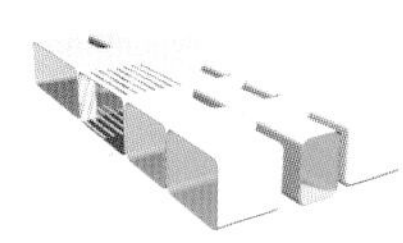
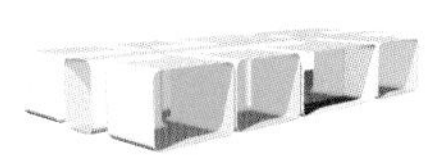

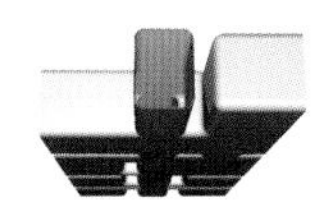
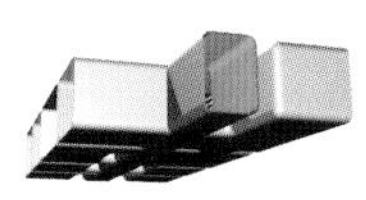

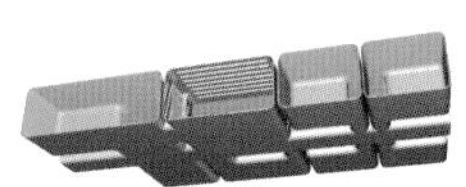

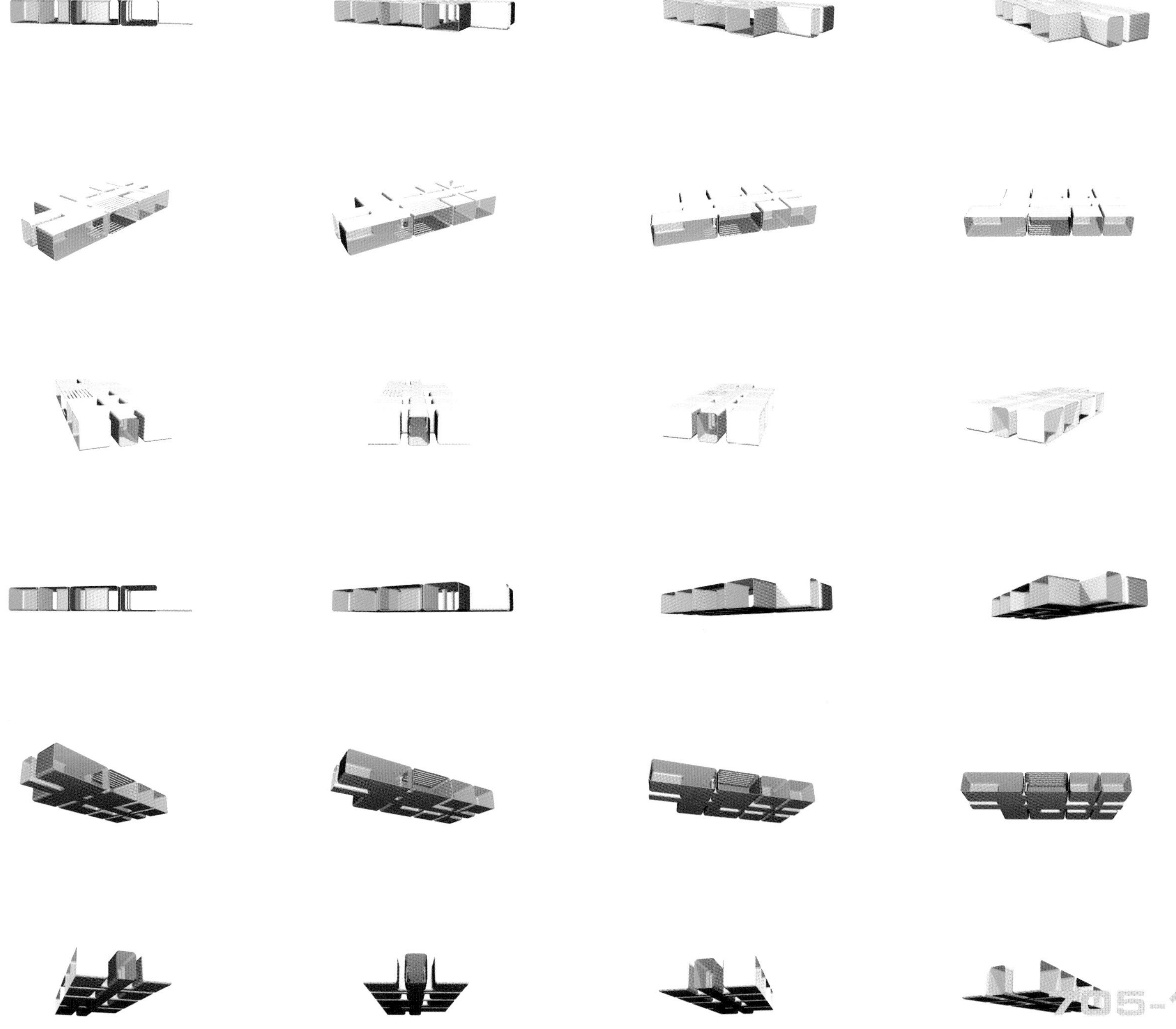

CAMERA TOUR OF THE BUILDING

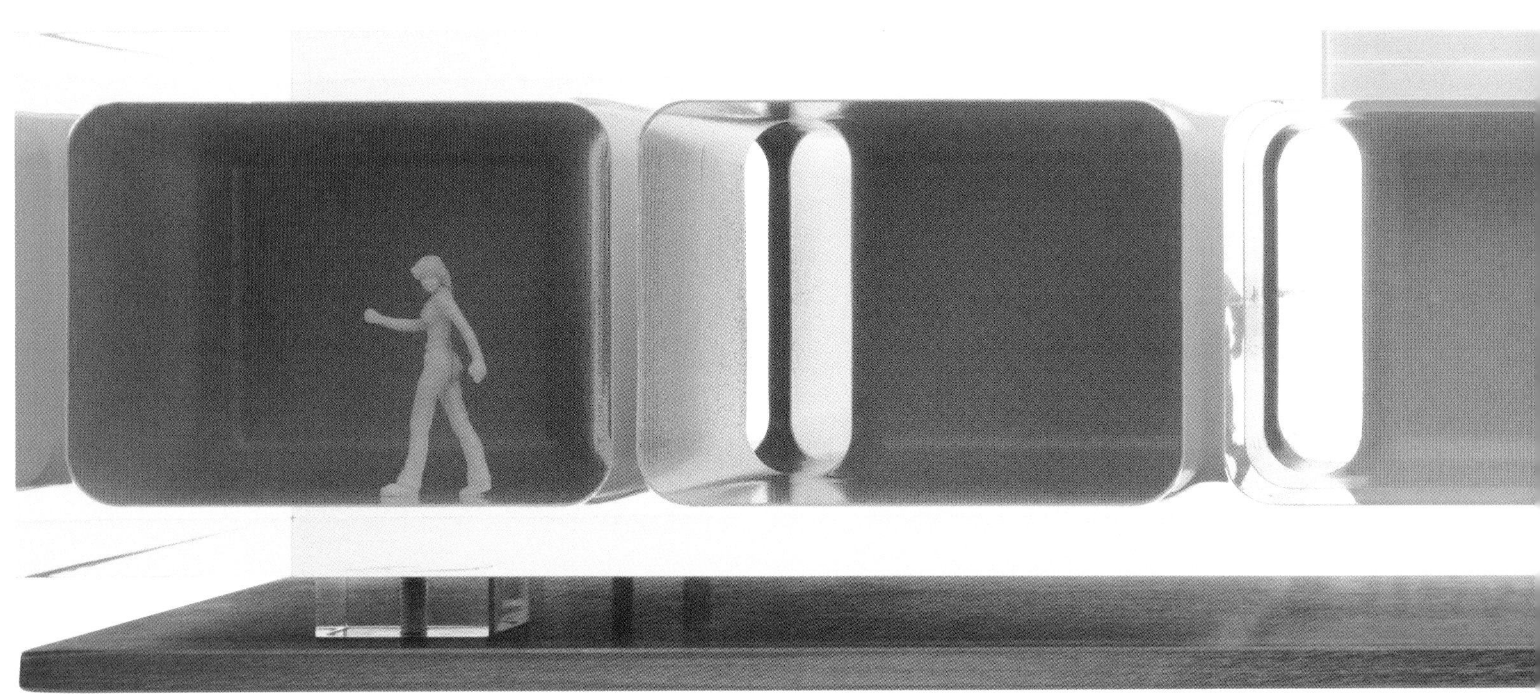

705-11

MODEL PHOTOGRAPH

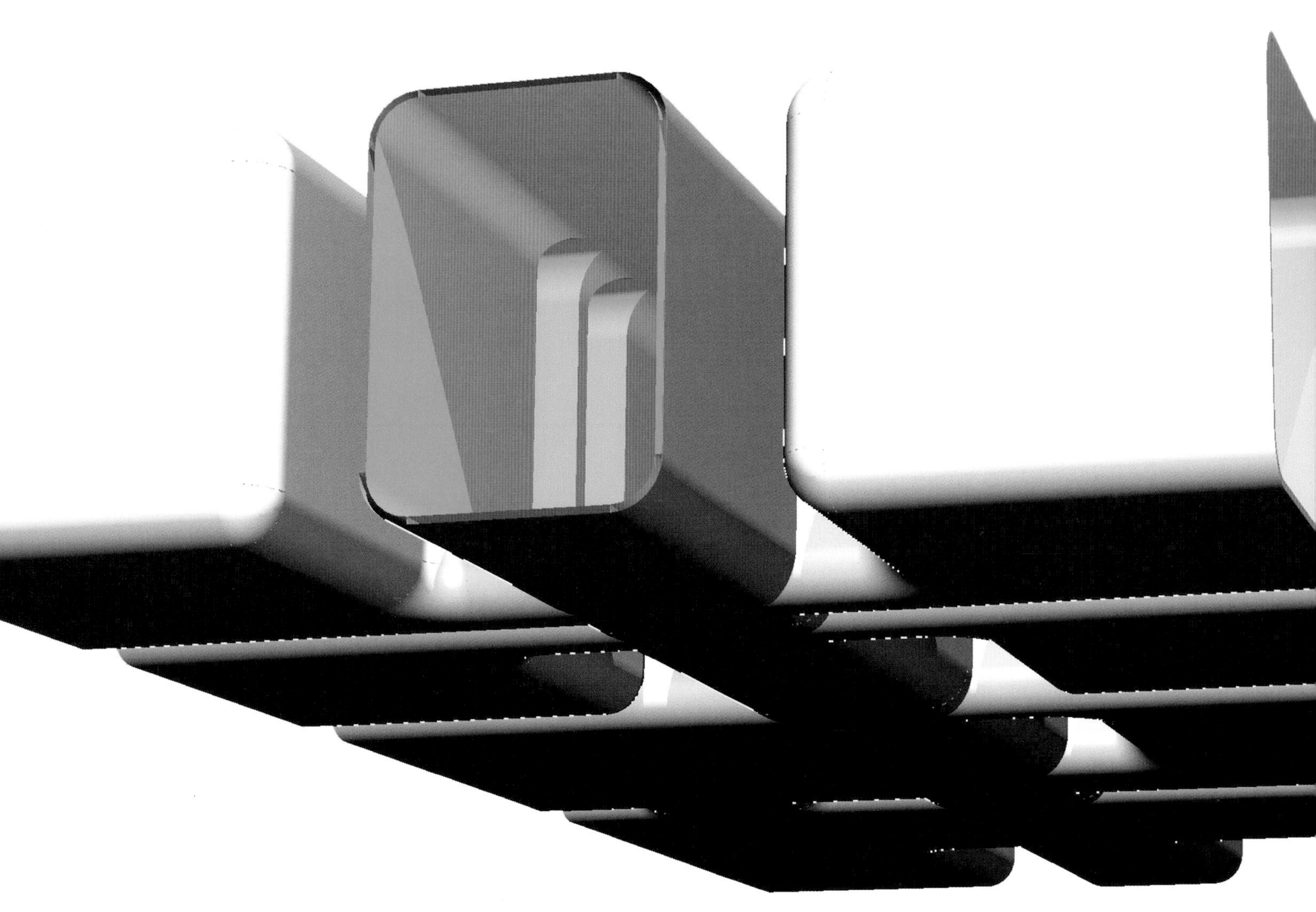

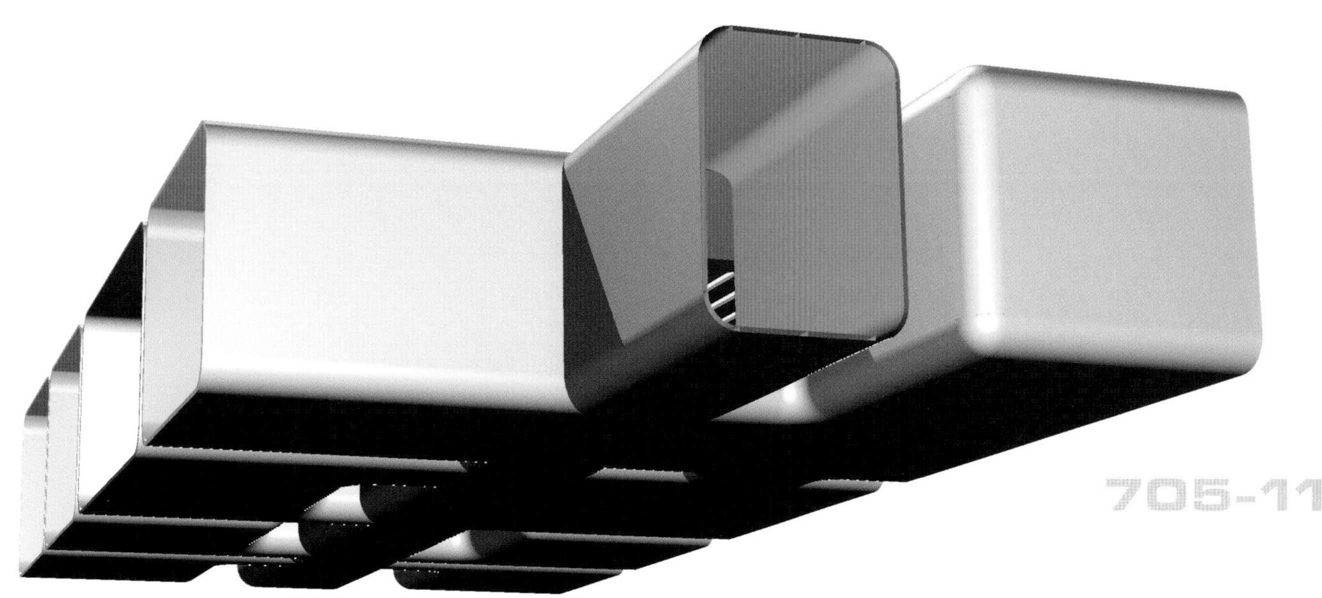
705-11

PROJECT DATA

SPORTS HALL / HALSTENBEK / 1993 DESIGN André Poitiers / Markus Röttger COLLABORATORS Göran Meyer / Carsten Kieselowsky / Ulrich Engel / Sabine Eisfeld
STRUCTURAL ENGINEERING Schlaich, Bergmann und Partner, Stuttgart MECHANICAL ENGINEERING Berneburg und Partner, Hamburg LANDSCAPE DESIGN Wehberg, Eppinger und Schm

X1 / HAMBURG / 1996 DESIGN André Poitiers / Martin Michel COLLABORATORS Ulrich Engel / Benjamin Holsten / Sabine Eisfeld

DONUT / BERLIN / 1997 DESIGN André Poitiers / Martin Michel COLLABORATORS Benjamin Holsten

PARISH CENTRE JOHNSALLEE / HAMBURG / 1997 DESIGN André Poitiers / Martin Michel / Uta Meins COLLABORATORS Jochen Dinkel / Ulrich Engel / Benjamin Ho
STRUCTURAL ENGINEERING Wetzel & von Seht, Hamburg MECHANICAL ENGINEERING Ridder und Meyn, Hamburg

PLASMA HOUSE / 1999 DESIGN André Poitiers / Martin Michel / Benjamin Holsten COLLABORATORS Jochen Dinkel / Ulrich Engel / Thomas Ladehoff

MM18-21 / YOKOHAMA / 2000 DESIGN André Poitiers / Martin Michel COLLABORATORS Ulrich Engel / Benjamin Holsten / Felix Schröder

SPORTS AND ART HOTEL / DÜSSELDORF / 2000 DESIGN André Poitiers / Ulrich Engel / Martin Michel COLLABORATORS Julia Banerjee / Florian Boxberg / Jochen D
ENVIRONMENTAL PLANNING Wehberg, Eppinger und Schmidtke, Hamburg

KAJEN / HAMBURG / 2000 DESIGN André Poitiers / Ulrich Engel / Martin Michel COLLABORATORS Jochen Dinkel / Bernd Fischer / Christian Greve / Benjamin Holsten / M

NEMOS HOUSE / BONN / 2000 DESIGN André Poitiers / Martin Michel COLLABORATORS Florian Boxberg / Jochen Dinkel / Ulrich Engel / Christian Greve / Benjamin Ho

BLIP / BONN / 2001 DESIGN André Poitiers / Martin Michel COLLABORATORS Jochen Dinkel / Ulrich Engel / Benjamin Holsten / Michael Kylies / Thomas Ladehoff

CAST HOUSE / 2001 DESIGN André Poitiers / Martin Michel COLLABORATORS Ulrich Engel / Bernd Fischer / Benjamin Holsten MODEL Michael Boje Modellbau

cke / Benjamin Holsten / Fabian Kremkus PROJECT MANAGEMENT Markus Röttger SITE MANAGEMENT Architekt BDA Rüdiger Franke, Hamburg
urg ACOUSTICAL ENGINEERING Tauber und Ruhe, Halstenbek

205-01

349-02

248-03

is Röttger MODEL Michael Boje Modellbau ENVIRONMENTAL PLANNING Wehberg, Eppinger, Schmidtke (WES + Partner)

238-04

702-05

310-06

ard Green / Benjamin Holsten / Michael Kylies / Thomas Ladehoff / Felix Schröder MODEL Michael Boje Modellbau

308-07

322-08

/ Thomas Ladehoff / Tarkan Tarbasar MODEL Michael Boje Modellbau

321-09

as Ladehoff MODEL Michael Boje Modellbau

351-10

705-11

OFFICE INFO / BIOGRAPHIES

ANDRÉ POITIERS, ARCHITEKT BDA RIBA STADTPLANER

Großer Burstah 36-38
Burstahhof
20457 Hamburg
T +49 (0)40 375 198 08/9
F +49 (0)40 375 198 21
E office@poitiers.de
www.poitiers.de

ANDRÉ POITIERS

1959 Born in Hamburg

1979-81 Apprentice cabinet-maker Asmus yachtbuilding yard Glückstadt

1981-83 Trained in banking Hamburger Sparkasse, Hamburg

1983-90 Studied architecture at the Technische Universität Braunschweig

1991-92 Sir Norman Foster London

1993-94 Design lecturer at the Technische Universität Braunschweig

Since 1995 Free-lance architect in Hamburg

1996 Member of the BDA

2000 Member of the Royal Institute of British Architects

2000 Registered as a town planner with the Hamburg Chamber of Architects

2000 First European Architects' Forum, Venice

ULRICH ENGEL

1967 Born in Hannover

1987-90 Apprentice cabinet-maker

1990-96 Studied architecture at the Technische Universität Braunschweig

Since 1996 Poitiers Architekten, Hamburg

MARTIN MICHEL

1969 Born in Westerland, Sylt, Germany

1990-97 Studied Architecture at Technische Universität Braunschweig

1993-95 Prof. Schulitz + Partner, Braunschweig

1995-97 Design / Private Practice

1996 First International Master Class, NAI, Rotterdam,
with Wiel Arets and Thom Mayne

1997-99 Sir Norman Foster, London

Since 1999 Poitiers Architekten, Hamburg

PUBLICATION LIST

BOOKS

Junge Beiträge zur Architektur Nelte Verlag, Wiesbaden, 1994
Architektur in Hamburg Jahrbuch der Architektenkammer Hamburg, 1995
Architektur in Schleswig-Holstein 1990-1996 Sporthalle Halstenbek, Junius Verlag, Hamburg, 1996
André Poitiers Projekte 1993-95 Book series with Ingenhoven, Overdiek und Partner – Düsseldorf / Bothe, Richter, Teherani – Hamburg / Becker Gewers, Kühn und Kühn - Berlin u.a., Nelte Verlag, Wiesbaden, 1996
Galerie AEDES Katalog, several projects, Aedes, Berlin, 1997
Wohnen in der Stadt – Wohnen in Hamburg, Leitbild, Stand, Tendenzen, Dölling und Galitz Verlag, Hamburg, 1997
Katalog-Buch zur Ausstellung des Bundes Deutscher Architekten Wohnen in der Stadt-Wohnen in Hamburg Lüdemannsches Grundstück, 1997
Katalog-Buch zur Ausstellung von Dirk Meyhöfer Rotterdam/Hamburg – Veränderungen am Strom, 1997
Architektur in Hamburg Jahrbuch der Architektenkammer Hamburg, 1997, Sporthalle Halstenbek
Eingang Weg + Raum Koch Verlag, Leinfelden-Echterdingen, 1998
Architektur in Hamburg Jahrbuch der Architektenkammer Hamburg, 1998
Architekur in Hamburg Jahrbuch der Architektenkammer Hamburg 1999, Brot und Spiele
Junge Deutsche Architekten 2, Angelika Schnell, book series, Birkhäuser-Verlag, Basel-Berlin-Boston, 2000
Restaurants, Cafés, Bars, Bettina Rühm, Callwey Verlag, München, 2001
André Poitiers 4 Shops, Kaye Geipel, Prestel Verlag, München-London-New York, 2001

MAGAZINES

Industriebau Autohaus der Zukunft, VAG, 04/88
autotektur 2000 Konzepte für das Autohaus der Zukunft, Quadrato Verlag, 1988
Förderpreis des Deutschen Stahlbaues 1990 1. Price Greenpeace - Basis Hamburg / 2. Price Kinderbibliothek an der Oker, Braunschweig, 08/90
db, Deutsche Bauzeitung Studenten-Werk / Greenpeace-Basis Hamburg / Diploma, Laves Price / Deutscher Stahlbau Förderpreis, 08/91
Glas, Architektur und Technik Ökonomisch und energiesparend Bauen / Niedrigenergie-Sporthalle, 09/95
DAB, Deutsches Architektenblatt Junge Büros berichten André Poitiers, Architekten BDA, Hamburg, 01/96
AIT, Architektur-Innenarchitektur Sporthalle Halstenbek, 01/96
DAB, Deutsches Architekten Blatt Neue Medien, 10/96
DBZ, Deutsche Bauzeitschrift Büro' 96 André Poitiers, 1996
ARKITEKTEN (Kopenhagen) André Poitiers, 1996
Art 4d (London/Bangkok) Something very unspecific, 10/97
Wettbewerbe Aktuell Landesvertretungen Niedersachsen Schleswig-Holstein in Berlin, 11/97
Bauwelt Die neuen Werkzeuge (CAD-Architektur), 11/97
ARCHITEKTUR + WETTBEWERBE Bauen für die Kirche Gemeindezentrum der Johannes-Kirche, Hamburg- Rotherbaum, 06/98
db, Deutsche Bauzeitung Alien - die Wiedergeburt Sporthalle Halstenbek, 07/98
DIE ZEIT, Magazin Nr. 37 Hier geht's rund! Doughnut, Headquarter of the Greens, Berlin, 09/98
DBZ, Deutsche Bauzeitschrift Büro-Spezial, 1998
Baumeister Junge Architekten in Deutschland, 1998
Bauwelt Die Wochenschau: Dat Backhus, 02/99
Detail Bäckerei-Café in Hamburg, 02/99
Lotus 100 New Pop Architecture, X-files. Unidentified Objects on Planet Architecture, Elemond S.p.A., Mailand, 1999
DBZ, Deutsche Bauzeitschrift Bäckerei und Café "Dat Backhus" – Alles im System, 10/99
Wettbewerbe Aktuell Regionalverwaltung Südwestmetall Reutlingen, 11/99
Baumeister Konzepte. Entwerfen zwischen Intuition und Vernunft, zwischen Zufall und Kalkül, 01/00
DAIDALOS Nr. 75 Das tägliche Brot, 06/00
DER ARCHITEKT Nr.10 Instant Architecture, 10/00
H.O.M.E. Das Magazin fürs Leben Architektur Hamburg, 12/00
FRAME, Nr. 19 "goodbye tante emma", 03/01

Baumeister B3 Digital: Effizientes Arbeiten mit 3D-Konstruktionen. 03/01
Domus Nr. 835 March 2001 Daily bread, Il pane quotidiano, 03/01
AMC n° 114 mars 2001 Plasma-house de l'objet–referent a la maison, 03/01
design report Nr. 4/01 Die 70er integriert
Restaurants, Cafés, Bars Bettina Rühm, Callwey Verlag, 07/01
AIT 9-2001 Lehrbeispiele, 09/01

EXHIBITIONS

1997 AEDES WEST
Galerie und Architekturforum, Berlin
1997 Wohnen in der Stadt – Wohnen in Hamburg
Exhibition by the Bund Deutscher Architekten
1997 Rotterdam/Hamburg – Veränderungen am Strom
Exhibition at NAi Rotterdam and in the Museum der Arbeit Hamburg
2000 HET STADION – The Architecture of Mass Sport
Exhibition at NAi Rotterdam
2001 Das Haus der Gegenwart
Exhibition by the SZ Magazin, Die Neue Sammlung - Staatliches Museum für angewandte Kunst, München
2002 Galerie AEDES, Berlin
"André Poitiers – Objects in the Territory"

BIOGRAPHIES OF THE AUTHORS

KRISTIN FEIREISS

1942 born in Berlin
1963-67 studied Art History at Johann Wolfgang Goethe University, Frankfurt, and Freie Universität Berlin
1967-80 Journalist for various cultural magazines and radio programs
1976-80 Editor, Internationales Design Zentrum Berlin
Editor "Werk und Zeit" magazine, Berlin
Board member, Deutscher Werkbund, Berlin
Founder and director of Aedes Gallery of Architecture, and start of the Aedes edition (until now more than 300 catalogues)
1988 Curator of the official architecture contributions for Berlin Cultural Capital of Europe. Touring exhibition: Berlin, Krakua, Kiev, Moscow, Bern, and Paris
1990 Initiator and curator of the exhibition "Paris, Architecture and Utopia", commissioned by the City of Paris, Pavillion d'Arsenal, Paris
1990-94 Editor Ernst & Sohn Publishers, Berlin
1991 Curator exhibition "Hans Poelzig Retrospective", Centre Pompidou, Paris
1992 Curator exhibition "Architectural Visions", Kunsthalle Hamburg
1993 Curator exhibition and public discussion "Das Schloß – against the reconstruction of Berlin City Castle"
1993 and 1994 Best Book Prize for the German speaking countries
1994 Medal of the Federal Republic (Bundesverdienstkreuz) for long and varied involvement in the promotion of architectural culture
1995 Co-founder and board member, Society for the Promotion of the Center for Science, Berlin
1995-97 Editor Wasmuth Publishers, Tübingen/Berlin
1995 Literature Prize for Building Culture 1995, from the Society of German Architects and Engineers (AJV)
1996 Founder of Aedes East, Hackesche Höfe, Berlin-Mitte
1996-97 Visiting Tutor, Humboldt University, Berlin, Institute for Cultural Research
1996-01 Director of the Netherlands Architecture Institute (NAi), Rotterdam
1996 Commissioner of the Dutch Pavilion Biennale, Venice
1997 Jury Rotterdam, Maaskantprijs
1998 Board Member of Kultur Ruhr GmbH c/o KVR, Essen
1999-0 Commissioner of the Dutch Pavilion Biennale, Venice
1999 Member of the Scientific Committee European Germany
2000 Chairman Architectuur Omgevings Prijs Nederland
2001 Jury Mies van der Rohe Award, Barcelona
2001 Verdienstkreuz am Band der Bundesrepublik Deutschland

THOM MAYNE

founded Morphosis in 1972 to develop an architecture that would eschew the normal bounds of traditional forms and materials and surpass the limiting dualism of modern and postmodern. As the firm steadily grows from 36 architects and designers, Mr. Mayne remains committed to the practice of architecture as a collective enterprise.

Born in Connecticut in 1944, Thom Mayne received his undergraduate degree from the University of Southern California in 1968. While there where he met five other students and educators with whom he would later join and create the Southern California Institute of Architecture, or SCI-Arc. In 1978, he received his Master's degree from Harvard University. Over the past 20 years, his academic activities have included teaching positions at Columbia University, Harvard University, Yale, the Berlage Institute in the Netherlands and the Bartlett School of Architecture in London. Currently, Thom Mayne holds a faculty position at UCLA School of Arts and Architecture. Each year, Thom lectures at approximately 15 international institutions and universities, as well as serving on multifarious architecture and design juries. Distinguished honors include the Rome Prize Fellowship from the American Academy of Design in Rome (1987), the Alumni of the Year Award from USC (1992), Member Elect from the American Academy of Arts and Letters (1992), and the 2000 American Institute of Architects/Los Angeles Gold Medal.

With Morphosis, Thom Mayne has been the recipient of 20 Progressive Architecture Awards, 39 AIA Awards and numerous other design recognitions. Under his direction, the firm has been the subject of various group and solo exhibitions around the world, most notably at the Contemporary Art Center in Cincinnati, Ohio, the Walker Arts Institute in Minneapolis, and a major retrospective at the Netherlands Architectural Institute (NAi) in 1999. In addition to these solo exhibitions, Morphosis has been included in prestigious group exhibitions. Drawings, furniture, and models produced by Morphosis are included in the permanent collections of such institutions as the MOMA, NYC, MOMA San Francisco, the MAK Vienna, The Israel Museum, Jerusalem, and the FRAC, France. The work produced by Morphosis is published extensively in prominent architectural publications worldwide.

ANDREAS RUBY

Born in 1966 in Dresden/Germany

ACADEMIC BACKGROUND

M.A. History of Art, Media Sciences and Philosophy, 1994, Humboldt University Berlin and University of Cologne.

• Visiting Scholar under Supervision of Bernard Tschumi, Columbia University New York, Graduate School of Architecture, Planning and Preservation, MSAAD Program

• Visiting Scholar under Supervision of Paul Virilio, Ecole Spéciale d'Architecture, Paris, 1993

PROFESSIONAL PROFILE

1 Architectural Criticism and Theory

• essays, reviews and studies for various architectural magazines such as DAIDALOS (Germany/USA), Bauwelt (Germany), Assemblage (USA), Archis (Netherlands), Architektur Aktuell (Austria), Werk, Bauen + Wohnen (Switzerland), and for exhibition catalogues, anthologies, books

2 Editorial production and consulting

• Executive Editor for Daidalos – Magazine for Architecture, Art and Culture, 1998-2000, Berlin

• Editorial Board Member of Werk, Bauen + Wohnen, the trilingual swiss architecture magazine, Zurich (2000-)

3 Symposium and Round-Table Discussion Moderation

Bauhaus Dessau, Dessau/Germany

• "Event Cities" (September 15./16th. 2000)

• "Urban Space vs. Urban Surface" (November 16th 1999)

• "Transparency in Modern Architecture" (July 2/3rd 1999)

• "Standardization in Modern Architecture" (August 6./7th 1999)

• Archilab, Orléans/France: 1999, 2000, 2001

• Graz biennal on media and architecture

• 5th Biennal, November, 7-11, 2001: "Imagineering the Urban Condition"

Berlin-Beta Festival, Berlin/Germany

• Berlin_Beta 3.0, "Virtual Mobility"

• Berlin_Beta 2.0, "Urban Drift"

4 Consulting

• programming consulting for architectural event series

• conceptual and strategic consulting for architects

5 Academic Acitivity

• Studio Instructor at Dessau Institute of Architecture at the BAUHAUS Dessau, Fall 2000

ALESSANDRO ROCCA

Milan based architectural writer, author and editor, published a large number of essays in "Lotus" and other Italian and international magazines and books. Gave lectures and participated at seminars and workshops in Italy and abroad.

1959 born in Genoa

1988 degree in architecture (University of Rome)

1990- editor of "Lotus international" architectural review, Electa

1991-92 post-lauream studies in Paris-Villemin university

1992 coeditor of "The Painted City. Genoa '92", Electa, Milan

1997 doctoral degree in Architecture, University of Genoa

1997 coeditor of "Fiere e città (Fairs and Cities)", Triennale di Milano/Charta, Milan

1998 editor of "Ian Ritchie", Motta, Milan / Whitney Library of Design, New York

1999 author of "Educatorium a Utrecht, Rem Koolhaas", Alinea, Florence

1999 author of "Atlante della Triennale", Triennale di Milano/Charta, Milan

2000 founder of the architectural research group "Alpha.ville"

2000- editor of "Lotus Navigator", architectural review, Electa

2000 author of "I limiti del museo (The limits of the museum)", Bologna University Press, Bologna

2000- teaches at the Polytechnic School of Milan

COLOPHON

TRANSLATION FROM GERMAN Michael Robinson
TRANSLATION FROM ITALIAN Christopher Huw Evans

GRAPHIC DESIGN Kitty Molenaar, Amsterdam

All illustrations are courtesy of André Poitiers.

All digital renderings in this book made by Benjamin Holsten.

PHOTOGRAPHS Friedrich Busam p. 41, 48/49, 188/189; Christoph Gebler p. 21, 24/25, 28/29, 72/73, 76/77, 102/103, 145; Leiska Photographie p. 130/131, 136/137, 138/139; Klemens Ortmeyer p. 30-35; André Poitiers p. 32, 33; Paul Schirnhofer inside cover; Reimer Wulf p. 36/37

A CIP catalogue record for this book is available from the Library of Congress, Washington, D.C., USA.

Deutsche Bibliothek Cataloging-in-Publication Data.

Poitiers, André: André Poitiers, objects in the territory / Andreas Ruby. Ed. by Kristin Feireiss. [Übers: Michael Robinson; Christopher Huw Evans]. - Basel; Boston; Berlin: Birkhäuser, 2002.

Printed on acid-free paper produced from chlorine-free pulp. TCF ∞
Printed in Belgium by Die Keure.

ISBN 3-7643-6617-6

www.birkhauser.ch
9 8 7 6 5 4 3 2 1